FREDERIC OZANAM AND HIS WORLD

Frederic Ozanam
AND HIS WORLD

Thomas E. Auge

THE BRUCE PUBLISHING COMPANY
MILWAUKEE

To the memory of my parents

Library of Congress Catalog Card Number: 66–15088

© 1966 THE BRUCE PUBLISHING COMPANY
MADE IN THE UNITED STATES OF AMERICA

Acknowledgment

I would be remiss if I did not acknowledge the assistance that I have received. Several of my colleagues on the Loras College faculty, Mr. Peter Beaves, Mr. Donald Schneider, Mr. Anton Slechticky, and Dr. Lawrence Moran read the manuscript at one stage or another of its development. All of them made corrections and improvements to it. Dr. Francis Lehner, also of Loras College, read the galley proofs and made numerous suggestions for improving the writing. I would also like to thank the typists who prepared the final draft. Obviously, I alone am responsible for any errors.

I am, however, most indebted to my wife, Theresa, for her assistance. Her patient, careful reading of the manuscript in its various forms and her intelligent criticisms of it were invaluable. Furthermore, it was her encouragement and interest which carried me over the difficult spots. It is a pleasure to acknowledge the important part that she played in the writing of the following pages.

*　　　*　　　*

Grateful acknowledgment is made to the following publishers for permission to quote from books published by them.

World Publishing Co., New York, N. Y., for permission to quote from the Meridian edition of Alexis de Tocqueville's *Recollections*.

Harper and Row Publishers, Incorporated, New York, N. Y., for permission to quote from Andre Maurois, *Lelia — The Life of George Sand*.

Benziger Brothers, Inc., New York, N. Y., for permission to quote from Monsignor Baunard, *Ozanam In His Correspondence*.

Introduction

Antoine-Frederic Ozanam is today a relatively obscure figure, known to the twentieth century primarily as the founder of the St. Vincent de Paul Society. Remarkably little has been written about him. The biographies that have appeared in English are either out of date or are unsatisfactory in one way or another. At the same time, historians of the nineteenth-century French Church, even those that concentrated upon the liberal Catholic movement in which Ozanam was so deeply involved, have given scant attention to him, choosing to dwell upon other personalities.

That Frederic Ozanam remains only a name to the twentieth century is both surprising and unfortunate, for his life exemplified to a high degree the ideal of the Christian layman. Here was a strongly religious man, whose life centered around his Christianity, living in the world as the head of a Christian family. Here also was an intellectual — a writer, a scholar, a teacher — eminently successful in an academic career at a secular university. Although he lived in a society that was increasingly hostile to Christianity, no man had less of the ghetto complex than he. He was neither a religious contemplative nor an ivory-tower scholar but was actively involved in the world and its problems.

Although there is need for a detailed, personal, day-by-day biography of Frederic Ozanam, this book is not intended to fill this need; rather the aim here is to examine the attitude and relationship of Ozanam to his society, to place in its social and intellectual setting the religious faith of this zealous Christian. Primarily, it is the effort of Ozanam to reconcile French Catholics to modern society that is the theme of these pages.

There are then two protagonists in this story: the man, Ozanam, and the world in which he lived. For us the most interesting aspect of this world is its modernity, for the environment in which Frederic Ozanam sought to realize the Christian ideal was much like our contemporary culture. It was a world full of violence and turmoil — secular, unstable, crisis ridden. It was a world of uncertainty and fear; nevertheless, and here is the key to Ozanam's life and thought, his attitude toward it was positive and open.

This question of the Christian's attitude toward his society was posed in new terms in the nineteenth century, posed in such a way, indeed, that the Christian churches have yet to give a final answer. Until the modern age French Catholics, and Western Christians as a whole, assumed that their culture was essentially Christian. From the fourth century, when Christianity was declared to be the official religion of the Roman Empire, it had remained the legal religion of most of Europe. The Protestant Reformation did not basically alter this; in fact it made those states that had continued in the Church more conscious of their Catholicity. It was the Enlightenment of the eighteenth century and the French Revolution that followed it which made visible the secular trends germinating beneath the surface of this Christian culture. Consequently, by 1831, when Ozanam first arrived in Paris, the culture of Europe and especially of France was strongly if not predominantly secular. Christianity was on the defensive against the encroachments of an aggressive and militant enemy. What response should the Church and the individual Catholic give to this new and threatening danger? Upon this question French Catholics were seriously and even bitterly divided between what has come to be called the conservative and liberal answers.

The position taken by each of these groups can be compared to the alternatives open to the defenders of a besieged city. For the conservative camp the strength of the enemy was so great and his weapons so diabolical that only by entrenching themselves more deeply within the walls of the citadel could they hope to withstand the attackers. Aside from occasional forays into the captured areas of the city, these Catholics wished to withdraw into the holy fortress to prepare grimly and pessimistically for the final onslaught of the enemy. The liberal Catholics, on the other hand, held that the Church, the holy fortress, should seek a reconciliation with those outside of its wall, since only in this way could Christians hope to reconquer the territory lost to the foe. The spirit of the liberal Catholics is best expressed by the words of one of its early leaders when he wrote as follows of secular liberalism, the symbol of anti-Catholicism: "You tremble before Liberalism. Very well. Catholicize it and society will be reborn."

Doubtless the terms conservative and liberal, because of their political connotations, are somewhat misleading. In nineteenth-century France, it is true, the division among Catholics did arise in part over political matters, but these were not the basic issues. As we have seen, essentially the quarrel was over the attitude to be taken toward the modern world. The alternatives posed were clear: to withdraw from the world or to seek a reconciliation with it; to maintain an unyielding front against the modern spirit or to search for new applications of Christian principles which would fit this spirit; to look to the past with nostalgia and to the present and future with pessimism or to hold that change and development are inevitable and thus to view the future with some optimism.

Of course the realities of life do not fit precisely these clear-cut alternatives, since advantages and dangers exist for the Christian on each side. If the conservative answer suffers from too little concern for the natural, from a pessimism that is hardly Christian, the liberal faces the danger of too great a stress upon the material, of an overly optimistic trust in human progress that does not agree with Christianity. Granted this, the problem of the attitude of the Christian to modern, secular society must still be answered.

Ozanam's response was consistently and emphatically liberal, a circumstance that put him out of step with the prevailing conservative mood of French Catholics. It was to be the major endeavor of his life to strive to bring the French Church to a more positive view of the modern world. For a time, in the years immediately prior to the revolution of 1848, the most fruitful and happy of Ozanam's life, it appeared that he and his liberal associates might succeed, but the tragic events of 1848 put an end to their hopes. Hence the story of Ozanam's liberal Catholicism is, in his lifetime, that of a failure, of an effort that fell far short of realization. In the long run, however, the hopes and ideals of Ozanam triumphed, for a century after his death the liberal Catholic movement has apparently come to be the predominant and prevailing sentiment of the Church and of Catholics.

Contents

Acknowledgment v

Introduction vii

I A Witness of Christianity 1

II A Network of Charity 20

III Rejoice in the Lord 43

IV The Sword of the Modern Age . . . 58

V The Cross at the Threshold of the Modern
World 79

VI Pass to the Side of the Barbarians . . . 98

VII A Charitable Agitation 113

VIII The Will of Providence 128

Index 147

xi

Chapter I A Witness of Christianity

In 1831 Frederic Ozanam, a young man of eighteen, arrived in Paris from his home in Lyon to study at the university. Almost immediately he became involved in the religious and intellectual controversies that were bubbling and seething in the cultural caldron that was Paris in the first half of the nineteenth century. In fact, within a few months he found himself the leader of a group of energetic, zealous Catholic students whose contributions to the Church they loved were both remarkable and permanent.

To the casual observer there was nothing in the appearance or background of the youthful Ozanam which would have set him apart from his fellow students. He was, in the great world of Paris, an obscure, shy student from the provinces. Of ordinary stature and figure, pale, with long, black, rather unkempt hair, he was not handsome nor were his gestures and bearing in any way elegant. His manner was that of the scholar, of one who spent his time in the study and the library; he had an abstract, introspective air, with the habit of casting his eyes downward as though absorbed in some profound intellectual problem.

1

Nor was his family background of importance in the cultured society of Paris. He came from an old Lyonnais family: solid, respectable people with a large number of lawyers and doctors in the family history. Important enough in Lyon, it was of little significance in the French capital. It was, however, through his Lyon connections that the young Ozanam gained entry into a circle of former residents of that city, older men who had achieved success in the intellectual world. Included in this group were the scientist, Ampere, and the writer, Ballanche, both of whom were to exercise an important influence upon Ozanam's life.

Furthermore, Ozanam did not come to Paris with the road paved by an already established intellectual or literary reputation. He had been a brilliant, precocious student of a renowned Lyon teacher, the Abbé Noirot, with whom he remained on intimate terms throughout his life. He had also published poetry and articles in Lyon periodicals, but these were mere boyish triumphs in the city of Hugo, Lamartine, and Chateaubriand.

He was in many ways a typical young man away from home for the first time: more brilliant, hardworking, and religious than most, but still a shy, homesick boy. His letters to his mother at this time show him to be melancholy and unhappy. Paris does not suit him; it is anti-Christian, unattractive. He is dissatisfied with his living quarters, since the other tenants are not the kind of people with whom he wishes to associate. His thoughts turn back to Lyon and the happy memories of his childhood.

But soon a change for the better occurs. The occasion for the improvement was a visit to the home of Andre Ampere. Ampere was an elderly man, famous for his achievements in science, the Newton of electricity, in the words of one writer. Ozanam had met him previously in Lyon, and once in Paris the young student paid a courtesy call on the older man. As a result of this visit, Ozanam was invited to make his home with the Ampere family. Doubtless this happy arrangement helped to reconcile the young man to Paris, but, more importantly, his acceptance into the Ampere household established a firm friendship between him and the family. The son, Jean-Jacques, a noted literary figure, was to be a lifelong friend of Ozanam and of great assistance later in the latter's academic career.

The two years during which the youthful Ozanam lived in close intimacy with the elder Ampere were satisfying and profitable ones for the young man. The supposed conflict between science and religion did not exist for Ampere, who was both a great scientist and a pious Catholic. He was also a great scholar with a wide range of interests and a deep fund of erudition. The strength of his memory was incredible. There is a story that on his deathbed one of those in attendance began to read from *The Imitation of Christ* to console the dying man. Ampere expressed his appreciation but added that there was no point in reading the book since he knew it all by memory. Certainly the influence of this wise, good man upon the young Ozanam must have been beneficial.

A student of his life will find yet another point of interest in his meeting with Ampere: namely, the strong impression the young man made on the older one. Judging from Ozanam's account, he knew Ampere only slightly before visiting him. Nevertheless, after only a brief conversation, this famous scientist offered to take into his home a young man whom he hardly knew. Clearly at eighteen, Frederic Ozanam was already a striking, attractive personality.

What were the qualities that attracted an elderly scholar and at the same time appealed to the youthful Catholic

students of Paris? All who knew Ozanam agree that it was
something inward, something intangible which shone through
the mediocre, ordinary outward appearance. One of his
friends described Ozanam's appeal as follows:

> He has the sacred fire. There is such an air of interior con-
> viction in this man, that without the appearance of doing so,
> he convinces and moves you.

Others write of his enthusiasm, of his ardent, kind nature,
and of his zeal. This shy, unprepossessing, sometimes dreamy
young man was fired with a devotion to truth and a love of
his fellow man. Neither the natural timidity of his nature,
nor the greatness of the individuals and the issues involved
would hinder him from speaking out, from acting as his
conscience dictated.

It was, primarily, his religious faith which aroused his
enthusiasm, animated his spirit, and moved him to action.
The eighteen-year-old Ozanam came to Paris, protected
against the corrosive acid of unbelief by a strong Catholicism,
the product of a childhood in a pious home. Both of Frederic's parents were deeply religious, constant in the practice
of their Christianity, in prayer, and in charitable work. So
strongly did the pulse of Catholicism beat within Frederic's
father that it overcame the flood of anti-Christianity which
swept over France during the revolutions of the 1790's. The
French republican armies of that period, in which the elder
Ozanam served with distinction, were violently hostile to
Catholicism and it is little less than a miracle that Frederic's
father came out of this experience with his religion intact.

Another incident of Ozanam's early days in Paris, trivial
and unimportant in itself, throws more light on his character.
Ozanam carried with him from Lyon a letter of introduction
to the most famous literary personality of the day, Chateaubriand, the author of the *Genius of Christianity*, the book

which began a religious revival in France. The young student was too shy to use the letter until he had been in Paris for some time. Once he had built up his courage to do so, Ozanam apparently made a favorable impression on the great Romantic writer, for when the interview ended, Chateaubriand invited the young man to attend the theater with him. Because he had promised his mother that he would not attend the theater, Ozanam had to refuse this gracious offer. Certainly an insignificant affair and one might be tempted to think that Ozanam was still in leading strings. At the same time one cannot help but admire the dutifulness and the strength of character required to turn down this invitation from a great, important person for what was a trifling, and to the sophisticated world of Paris, laughable reason. Surely Ozanam was no ordinary eighteen-year-old student.

The best evidence of his strength of character, of his zeal for the good, of his deep religious commitment is to be found in his reaction to Paris. Upon his arrival there, this young provincial found himself in the midst of a hostile, tumultuous environment, a difficult, even dangerous society for a Christian. The response to this secular world by Ozanam and those Catholic students who joined him was to seek to be living "witnesses of Christianity." To understand the significance of the achievements of these young students, to appreciate the positive nature of their response, a few comments on the intellectual and religious situation they faced will be necessary.

The Paris into which Ozanam stepped in 1831 was physically an old city: dark, dirty, and crowded. It was the exotic, mysterious metropolis with narrow streets and alleys, cul-de-sacs, garrets, and cellars, which Balzac and Eugene Sue peopled with the creatures of their vivid, fertile imaginations.

Problems of city government, lighting, urban renewal, all had to await the reforming zeal of Napoleon III, who in the 1850's built modern Paris with its spacious boulevards, parks, and beautiful gardens. The medieval nature of the Paris of Ozanam's day is shown by a cholera epidemic that struck during his first years there, since before the advent of public sanitation the old, dirty cities of Europe were periodically visited by the plague.

If Paris was in appearance an old city, this was misleading, for underneath the surface great changes were occurring which made the world of Ozanam modern. It was a society in transition, on the move from the rural, aristocratic culture of the Old Regime of the eighteenth century to the urban, mass world of today. Change was everywhere, political and economic instability endemic. In this shifting maelstrom of development, the problems of the modern world were beginning to appear. Thus behind the smiling face of material progress lurked violence and chaos. Revolutions, street disturbances, terroristic activities, and industrial unrest were common occurrences in the France of Ozanam's day. Indeed, the year before Ozanam arrived in Paris, in July, 1830, an uprising in the streets of Paris had forced the legitimate Bourbon king, Charles X, into exile. Unfortunately, the revolution that overthrew the king was aimed as much at the Catholic Church.

The reasons for this are not difficult to find. The circumstances of the first great French Revolution (that of 1789) were such that the revolutionaries and the Church went in opposite directions. Consequently, those who supported the ideals of the revolution were hostile to the Church, while Catholics, as a whole, were sympathetic to the legitimate monarchy and the pre-1789 Old Regime.

The reign of Charles X added to this animosity. Charles,

the brother of the unfortunate Louis XVI who was executed by his subjects in 1793, was reactionary in politics and stanchly Catholic in religion. As a young royal prince in the halcyon days before 1789, he had led a luxury-loving, even immoral life, but the tribulations of exile as well as advancing age had made him sincerely religious. Hence, when he came to the throne, he cemented more firmly than ever the so-called "union of altar and throne." For example, Charles revived all medieval religious ceremonial in his coronation, including the laying on of the hands of the newly anointed king to cure the sick. Once in power, Charles, among other things, made sacrilege a major crime, punishable by death. Education was placed in the hands of the Church, censorship of the press and of literature was extensive. King and Church acted as if the anti-Christian Enlightenment and the French Revolution of 1789 had never occurred. For them France remained a Catholic nation when in fact it was, intellectually at least, pluralist if not secular.

As a result of the tie of the Church with the unpopular monarchy, anticlericalism, if not hatred of Christianity, was rampant in the Paris of 1831. A priest could not appear in the streets of the city in clerical dress without danger of insult. In the disturbances that followed the July Revolution of 1830 seminaries were attacked in several provincial cities. Some bishops, fearful of the hatred of the people because of their identification with the monarchy of Charles X, fled the country or went into hiding. The climax of this anticlericalism was reached in 1831 when a mob sacked the residence of the Archbishop of Paris. The occasion of this riot was a royalist ceremony held in a church in Paris. Provoked by this imprudent action, a wild anticlerical mob demolished in a frenzy the episcopal palace. Not only were the household goods of the archbishop destroyed, but works of art and precious manuscripts were lost. For days fishermen pulled debris from the Seine River. The hatred and violence of the mob were so extreme that it was barely prevented from tearing down the crosses from the cathedral of Notre Dame. The government of King Louis-Philippe, which had replaced that of Charles X, did nothing to prevent the destruction since it too had anticlerical propensities. The liberal Catholic nobleman, Montalembert, describes for us how he stood under arms as a member of the National Guard far from the scene of the riot, futilely awaiting orders to intervene while the Seine carried past him the fragments from the ruin of the archbishop's palace. Montalembert's condemnation of the Catholic royalist who brought this upon the Church by associating it with the monarchy is just. He wrote: "It has been your doing: you fastened your *fleur-de-lis* to a crucifix, and the people have protested against this union with a sacrilege."

It is not surprising that the pious Ozanam was appalled by the hostility to Christianity that he discovered in Paris. It was one of the reasons for his early dislike of the city. He wrote to his cousin, Ernest Falconnet, a month or so after his arrival: "Paris displeases me because there is no life, no faith, no love; it is like a corpse to which I, young and alive, am attached. . . ."

Anti-Christian sentiments were nowhere stronger than in the academic, intellectual circles. The novelist Stendhal announced with assurance in 1822 that Christianity would be dead within twenty-five years. Doubt, skepticism, and unbelief were dangers faced by all young Catholics. Secular religions, to replace Christianity, were preached throughout Paris by self-appointed messiahs. Among the welter of natural, social, humanitarian doctrines offered as an improvement on the out-of-date, traditional, spiritual Catholicism were the "new Christianity" of the Saint-Simonian Utopian Socialists and the Positivist "religion of humanity" of Auguste Comte.

No wonder that many young Catholics, growing up in such an atmosphere, found themselves succumbing to doubt. The philosopher, Jouffroy, a leading professor at the Sorbonne during Ozanam's student days, has described in a melancholy passage how, at the age of twenty-two, he suddenly, sadly realized that he had lost his faith. A younger contemporary of Ozanam's, Ernest Renan, has pictured for us how skepticism eventually came to dominate his mind, this during the period while he was studying at the seminary. Ozanam himself was threatened by this almost overwhelming current of unbelief. At the age of sixteen he experienced a religious crisis which, with the aid of his teacher, Abbé Noirot, he was able to overcome. Doubtless the roots of his religious belief, planted in a pious Christian family environment, were too deep and alive to be killed by this disease of doubt, but it is indicative of the strength of the anti-religious current of the day that one such as he could be threatened.

Such was the world in which the Catholic student lived in the Paris of 1831: a world in which religion was held up to scorn, derided as superstition, or written off as an interesting anachronism. It was not enough that these young students were threatened by secular, materialistic intellectual onslaughts; they had also to put up with other annoyances. The government of Louis-Philippe suspected all Catholics of wishing to restore the legitimate monarchy so that these Catholic students found themselves spied upon by government agents. Still more difficult to bear was the hostility and mistrust of other Catholics. The liberal Catholic movement of Lamennais and the newspaper *L'Avenir* was at its height at this time, causing bitter controversy among French Catholics. Ozanam, in a letter written to his mother in 1834, spells out the difficulties facing these Catholic students:

> We are surrounded by political parties who, because we are coming of age, want to draw us in their armies: even in religion, we hear only controversy, we see disputes where charity is lacking and much scandal given. There is no literary meeting at which spies of the government or of certain so-called religious periodicals might not be present. [We are] called bigots by our unbelieving fellow students, liberal and reckless by older people, questioned at every turn upon our thoughts and actions, [and are] under the arbitrary power of our university professors; [we] have to fear for ourselves during the street fighting and especially for our relatives who are far away.

What was the reaction of this enthusiastic, ardent young Catholic to all of this? Many, if not most of his fellow Catholics, stubbornly and intransigently fought back. Theirs was essentially a defensive position; they were clear and definite on the flaws and weaknesses of their society and of their opponents, but they were not strong in the Christian response to the challenge of the nineteenth century. Ozanam, particularly in his younger days, shared this defensive mentality; thus much of his early writing was attacks on opponents of the Church, e.g., Protestantism, socialism, rather than a positive presentation of his beliefs. But even at this time this was not enough for Ozanam. This obscure, retiring student, surrounded by a hostile world, did not withdraw from it, did not reject and condemn it; instead he endeavored to stand as a living witness of the truths of Christianity in the midst of a secular society.

Ozanam understood well the nature of unbelief in the modern world. Many fanatical, vitriolic foes of religion can be found around us, but these the Christian can meet and deal with. By their very hatred of religion, by their willingness to engage in controversy over it, these open enemies are psychologically and intellectually in a position that can be combated. Hence it is the duty of the Christian to prepare himself by education and learning for this combat. This we shall see was a constant theme in Ozanam's thought, namely, the obligation of the Christian to engage in intellectual controversy with the anti-Christian elements in his society.

But a more subtle, pernicious poison to religion in the modern world is the bland, passive indifference of most nonbelievers. Religion, to them, is of such little significance that it is not worth considering. It was just such disinterest in spiritual matters that Ozanam found among the Parisian students. These non-Christian students, he wrote in a private letter, did not contradict the arguments of Catholic students, but these arguments had no effect upon them; they changed neither their actions nor their attitude toward religion. It was the futility of intellectual controversy in overcoming this indifference which convinced Ozanam of the importance of example as a possible means of influencing the non-Christian, hence his desire to be a witness of the truths of his faith.

Ozanam was joined in these two endeavors — to combat the anti-Christian attacks and to serve as a living example of Christianity — by a number of his fellow students. His achievements in these four years — 1831 to 1835 — are really those of himself and his friends; they are the work of a group, not of any individual. Ozanam, it is true, as his friends willingly admit, was the leader. One of them wrote that "he was easily with us *primus inter pares*"; nevertheless the contributions of the others cannot be ignored.

For the most part they were a group of unknown, insignificant, provincial students, a fact that makes their accomplishments the more remarkable. The group included

Letaillandier, Lamarch, Devaux, Cleve, among others, names of no import to us. Among the group, however, there is one who deserves notice: Lallier, Ozanam's closest friend and eventually the godfather of his daughter. He too, like Ozanam, was preparing for a legal career, and after completing his studies returned to his home at Sens where he became a successful, important figure. He remained, throughout his life, active in Catholic social work, especially in the St. Vincent de Paul Society, and wrote occasionally for Catholic periodicals.

Lallier shared Ozanam's zeal and piety, being apparently second only to his friend in influence and leadership among Catholic students. He was in personality a perfect counterweight to the mercurial, emotional Ozanam, described by those who knew him as a serious, reserved person who provided balance and stability to the group. So mature and stolid did Lallier appear to his young friends that they dubbed him "Father Lallier."

The first meeting of these two zealous Catholics set the tone for their lifelong friendship. Both were attending a lecture at the *College de France* where the speaker was indulging in the popular pastime of ridiculing Christian doctrine, in this case the Book of Genesis. Lallier resented this strongly and looking around the audience noticed another young man who obviously felt as he. After the lecture Lallier sought out the other, who was, of course, Ozanam, and introduced himself. This first meeting was prophetic, for they remained devoted friends and collaborators in the defense of their religion.

This group of students was not alone in its efforts, for older men, important literary and religious figures, supported them. Chateaubriand and Ballanche, the latter originally from Lyon, gave Ozanam and his group encouragement and inspiration. The youthful Count Montalembert, already famous for his battles on behalf of free teaching, was in sympathy with them, and Ozanam attended intellectual gatherings in his apartment. Another influence was the Abbé Gerbet, a noted Catholic writer and intellectual, an associate of Lamennais in the liberal Catholic movement, who delivered a series of lectures on philosophy of history which stimulated Ozanam and others of his group.

Of the older men who contributed to the achievements of these students it was the editor of an obscure periodical by the name of Bailly who supplied the most material and practical assistance. Over the years this man had given of his time and his means to aid Catholic students in Paris. Ozanam's older brother, Alphonse, had benefited from this some years before. Bailly ran a *pension* for the students, established a reading room in his place of business, and organized study groups. His influence upon Ozanam and his friends was direct and important, especially in the foundation of the St. Vincent de Paul Society. It was his residence where the first meeting was held, and he was for sixteen years its first president. Appropriately enough, Bailly remains known to history only through his connection with the St. Vincent de Paul Society.

The first activities of Ozanam and his friends, although not particularly important in themselves, are indicative of their state of mind. Along with the duty of serving as an example of Christian living, these young men also considered that it was their responsibility to defend their religion against the intellectual attacks to which it was constantly subjected. To fulfill this task knowledge was required; hence study groups were organized, papers were prepared, and lectures

delivered. It was not simply, or even primarily, a matter
of the study of theology, for history, philosophy, and economics also occupied their attention.

The opportunity to apply this knowledge, to put to use
the fruits of these Catholic study groups came in debates
with rationalist fellow students. Apparently the Catholic students at the University of Paris found themselves involved
in passionate arguments over religion. Finally it was suggested that formal debates be held, with Bailly's place of
business as the scene of battle. A series of lengthy, sharp
intellectual jousts, with Ozanam as the Catholic champion,
were held. Very likely little was settled, probably few opinions were altered; nevertheless how typical was this approach
for Ozanam. For him the truths of Christianity were such
that they could hold their own in open debate, with those
in disagreement having the right to speak. Free and open
discussion was for Ozanam the only Christian answer to the
opponents of Catholicism; force, personal condemnation,
and invective had no place in his view of controversy.

More serious than the derogatory comments of fellow
students were the attacks made upon Catholicism from the
lecture platforms of the university where the prevailing
sentiment was un-Christian. Catholic students had to endure
sarcasm and open criticism of revelation, of miracles, and
of the union of the Church with the monarchy. A person
so committed to Catholicism as Ozanam could not passively
endure such attacks, a mind so open to discussion and to
the free play of ideas could not fail to respond to such
one-sided arguments. Although his determination to oppose
publicly these assaults on his religion was in part a defensive
reaction, it was also something more. It was a part of his
effort to be a witness of Christianity, for his goal was not
so much to refute his opponents as to show, in his words,

"that it is possible to be Catholic and to have common sense, that it is possible to love religion and liberty."

How could a student with the purely passive role of listening to the lecture answer the attacks of a professor? The most common method with French students is to organize disturbances in the lecture room. Organized clapping of the hands, booing, shouting have been and are yet today recognized methods of indicating disapproval of a professor. Ozanam, at least indirectly, had to put up with this himself when he became a member of the faculty of the university. It is testimony to the courtesy and confidence of Ozanam and his fellow Catholic students that they did not stoop to such anarchial practices; instead Ozanam, on several occasions, prepared a paper in which the anti-Christian remarks of the professor were answered. This was then sent to the individual concerned with a courteous covering letter requesting that it be read to the lecture audience. Usually, and it is a credit to the open-mindedness of these scholars, the professor read Ozanam's answer to his students.

Only once did the offender ignore the letter from Ozanam; a professor of philosophy, a former Catholic, and one of the most illustrious members of the faculty, Jouffroy, had struck at the element of revelation in Christianity. He had also suggested that Christianity was extinct, that it would be replaced by a new religion, more in touch with progress and modern times. Ozanam wrote a polite refutation which Jouffroy promised to read but never did. Ozanam wrote again with the same result. Finally, a protest was prepared which was signed by fifteen students before being sent to Jouffroy. This time the professor read Ozanam's answer and publicly apologized for having angered anyone by his remarks. He was, according to Sainte-Beuve, who knew him, a pleasant, amiable man. Jouffroy concluded with the significant comment that in the past criticism of his lectures had come entirely from the side of rationalism, but now, for the first time, the opposition was Catholic. Though this affair was trifling, still it was clear that these young Catholic students had already gained some success in their endeavor to improve the position of the Church in a hostile world.

Shortly after this incident they took a further step. Three of them, of whom one was Ozanam, presented a petition signed by one hundred students to the archbishop of Paris, de Quelen. It stated that Paris was the scene of a violent controversy over religion, that the Church was assaulted from the lecture platform, in books, and in pamphlets. The students suggested that a series of Lenten sermons be preached from Notre Dame to answer this flood of anti-Christian propaganda. Archbishop de Quelen, a conservative prelate, received them courteously and listened patiently to their views. But when the young men suggested certain individuals as most fitted to preach the sermons, the archbishop put them off. Eventually the Lenten sermons were preached in Notre Dame by seven men chosen by the archbishop, none of whom had been on the students' list, and as a result, perhaps, they were not particularly successful.

The next year, 1834, the twenty-one-year-old Ozanam, this time accompanied by Lallier and another student, was back again with a petition signed by two hundred students. It contained a sentence that illustrated perfectly what these young men sought. It went as follows:

> Therefore, your Grace, we had desired someone, who without losing time in refuting arguments that are today out of date, would display Christianity in all of its grandeur, and in harmony with the aspirations and necessities of man and society.

In other words, give us sermons that are positive rather than negative, that appeal to the society in which they are delivered. Although this was not included in the petition, the committee of three students also made clear that Père Lacordaire, a noted preacher with strong liberal sentiments, was in their minds the only man fitted to deliver these sermons, if they were to succeed.

Once again the elderly, aristocratic archbishop listened politely; once again he failed to follow the suggestions made by the students. It was not until the Lent of 1835, a year later, that Archbishop de Quelen decided to give in and to permit Lacordaire to be the preacher. The sermons of Lacordaire were all that Ozanam and his friends had hoped they would be, with the cathedral regularly crowded and with many non-Catholic intellectuals in attendance. So successful were the sermons that they became an annual affair with Lacordaire delivering them until he left Paris, after which a famous Jesuit preacher, Père Ravignan, took over the pulpit. According to Ozanam, the Lenten sermons preached by these two men were responsible for many conversions to Catholicism.

Père Lacordaire, who was to be the restorer of the Dominican Order to France, was in 1835 not yet a member of this order. He was, however, already well known for his participation in the liberal Catholic movement centering around the journal, L'Avenir. At this time he was still a young man, some ten years older than Ozanam, with whom he had been friendly since shortly after the latter's arrival in Paris. Over the years the friendship grew, although it was not so much a personal, intimate relationship, such as Ozanam had with Lallier, as a common collaboration in the difficult task of reconciling the Church to the modern world. For twenty years, from their first meeting in 1833 until Ozanam's death in 1853, these two energetic, able men worked closely together with little or no disagreement as to policies or principles.

Père Lacordaire was, in the opinion of Sainte-Beuve, the greatest preacher of the age. The latter, driven by the insatiable curiosity which characterized him, attended the Lenten sermons, which he found most attractive. Lacordaire spoke, so writes Sainte-Beuve, the language of the nineteenth century to the men of the century, especially the words, the images, and the poetry of the students of the day. Today the printed words of Lacordaire have little life; for us his sermons are too rhetorical, too flowery, too emotional, but at the height of the Romantic movement, they struck exactly the right note. Furthermore, Lacordaire was apparently able to capture his listeners by his enthusiasm and his personality. He possessed the intangible quality of all great orators, the charismatic gift of personal magnetism. Thus Ozanam had his wish: a preacher who presented the truths of Christianity in the center of Paris, not in a negative, out-of-date manner, but in a modern, positive, attractive, even beautiful fashion.

Before leaving this contribution of Ozanam and his friends to the improvement of the position of the French Church, there are certain things in it that tell us of Ozanam himself. In the first place, his constant stress upon the positive should be noted, for it is not a defense of the Church that is sought but an attractive presentation of its truths. Here again we find Ozanam's confidence that the beauty and truth of Christian dogma, presented in an open, public manner, are the best means of defending and promulgating it; certainly the success of Lacordaire did not disprove his contention.

It is also of interest to note the zeal and the courage of Ozanam and his friends. These young Catholic students have the temerity to present suggestions to the most important prelate in France, and when he does not follow their advice, to return once again with further suggestions. This is especially noteworthy when the retiring, reserved character of Ozanam is remembered. That it was not easy for Ozanam to undertake such activities was shown when, many years later, he wrote to Lallier of how frightened they were as they approached the archbishop's residence. That this shy, scholarly, introspective young man would lead such a campaign is testimony of the strength and zeal of his faith. Indeed, the youthful Ozanam, as a student in Paris, is the best proof of his aphorism that "religion leads less to thought than to action."

Chapter II A Network of Charity

By far the outstanding example of the efforts of these young men to be living witnesses of Christianity was the foundation of the St. Vincent de Paul Society. Founded in 1833 by Ozanam and his friends, the Society at the time of his death twenty years later had spread all over the world.

The impetus for the organization of this Society arose out of the occasional meetings of a small group of students at the home of the journalist, Bailly, for the purpose of discussion and study. Eventually, in May, 1833, these seven or eight students decided to form themselves into an association that would meet regularly to perform some spiritual exercises: readings, prayers, and discussion. Also, it was agreed, they would each contribute to a fund which would be distributed personally to the poor by members of the Society. It was, then, to be a religious organization whose purpose was to advance the spiritual life of its members, primarily through the practice of charity to the poor.

Although Ozanam is usually referred to as the founder of the Society, he was no more the initiator than any of the others. He himself, with his usual modesty, gives the credit to others. In 1844, in an obituary for his older friend, Bailly, Ozanam assigns the honor of founder to him. Here Ozanam states that Bailly had called together a group of students to whom he suggested that they hold regular meetings for charitable purposes under the patronage of St. Vincent de Paul. It is possible that Ozanam exaggerated Bailly's importance here in an effort to honor the memory of his recently deceased friend, but regardless of the complete accuracy of Ozanam's statement of 1844, it is clear that Bailly made an important contribution to the formation of the St. Vincent de Paul Society. It was under his aegis that these young men originally met, and it was at his residence that the first meetings of the Society were held. Furthermore, it was through the elder man's connections that the group was put in touch with the poor. Through Bailly the students became acquainted with a Sister Rosalie, who had given her life to the poor of Paris. Because of her reputation among the lower classes as well as through her knowledge of the conditions in the slums of the city, the St. Vincent de Paul Society was quickly and usefully engaged in charitable work. Finally, Bailly served for years as the first president of the group.

At other times, however, Ozanam gives credit for the suggestion that they form the St. Vincent de Paul Society to a student friend, Letaillandier. He wrote this many years later, but it may well be that Letaillandier was indeed the first to propose such an organization; still it would be wrong to assign the honor of founding the Society to any one of the group. It was a communal enterprise that grew out of their common faith and aims. The comment of Lamarck, one of the original seven or eight, is perfectly accurate: "To tell the truth, not one of us, not even Ozanam, who certainly had the greatest initiative and the most ardent zeal, could be described as the founder of the Society of St. Vincent de Paul."

Nevertheless Ozanam more than anyone else deserves the title of founder if by this is meant he who created the vast, international, charitable organization which the St. Vincent de Paul Society eventually came to be. Perhaps it was Bailly, perhaps Letaillandier, perhaps another member of the group who suggested that they form themselves into a spiritual society. In any case there is no evidence that anything was originally envisioned beyond an organization of Paris students. The first meeting in May, 1833, was indeed the seed out of which grew the great tree that is today the St. Vincent de Paul Society, but whoever planted the seed did not realize the life that was in it. The true founder of the Society was he who saw the possibilities contained in the coming together of this small group of students; to return to the metaphor, the one responsible for the great tree, with its innumerable branches, which has thrown the beneficent shadow of charity over the whole world was not the planter of the seed, who did not realize what he was doing, but he who nourished it with his zeal and watered it with his hopes. If any of the group deserves this honor, it is Frederic Ozanam.

But to be more accurate this is giving Ozanam too much credit, since the transition of the Society from a small group of friends to an international organization was almost accidental. For a Christian, God would have to be, in a more direct sense than is usually meant, the founder of the St. Vincent de Paul Society, as there is something providential in its rapid, almost incredible growth. It became the greatest lay organization in the Catholic Church without anyone originally intending it be so, without any forethought, any plan of development to follow. And it did so overnight, against the efforts of important groups and individuals within the Church.

The accidental character of the transition of the Society from an association of friends to a universal body is shown by a debate which took place at a meeting of the Society in May, 1834. A year after its founding the Society had become so popular among the Catholic students of Paris that the numbers in attendance at the meetings precluded the close, intimate atmosphere which had previously been present. It was suggested, therefore, that the group should divide into several smaller units or conferences, united together by common rules of procedure as well as by similar spiritual and charitable practices. Occasionally general meetings of the whole Society would be held, but, for the most part, each conference would meet and act separately. This proposal caused a lengthy, serious, and, for these religious young men, bitter debate. Eventually the principle of division into smaller conferences won out, but it is significant that such a fundamental organizational principle was not suggested until a year after the Society was formed and that it was received then with considerable skepticism. Had the proposal not carried it is unlikely that the Society founded by Ozanam and his friends would ever have been more than a student society at the University of Paris.

The haphazard, gradual development of the original Society into the international body that it came to be is also indicated by the method by which its rules of organization and procedure were adopted. Many of them, for example, resulted from the correspondence between Lallier and Ozanam in the years immediately subsequent to the latter's return to Lyon. Lallier at this time was the secretary of the Society, while Ozanam was the president of the Lyon con-

ference. The letters that passed between these two young
friends contain constant discussion of the problems faced
by the struggling infant organization. Out of these discussions came many suggestions which were to be incorporated
into the first manual of the Society prepared by Lallier and
Bailly.

The key step in the conversion from a Parisian student
group into first a national then an international organization
was the foundation of new conferences outside of Paris. The
first of these were the creation of students who, having completed their studies in Paris, had returned to their homes
in the provinces. There is good evidence that Ozanam was
the source of this fundamental development. A young man
by the name of Curnier, who founded in the city of Nimes
the first conference outside of Paris, wrote to Ozanam as
follows:

> It was with sincerity that I promised you when I left that I
> would try to form at Nimes an association similar to that
> which you founded in Paris. You expressed to me the desire
> of seeing France enveloped in a network of charity, and you
> have infused into me some of the ardent zeal which animates
> you.

"A network of charity" that will envelope not only France
but the whole world in its loving, benevolent strands, this
is the dream which created the St. Vincent de Paul Society,
the dream of Frederic Ozanam. He had not only the dream
but the energy and the initiative to make it a reality, and
throughout his life, indeed up to the present day, Ozanam
has been, as he was in 1834 for Curnier, the example that
has given life to his Society.

The appeal of the St. Vincent de Paul Society to Catholics
of the nineteenth century was instantaneous and extensive.
By 1855, two years after Ozanam's death and twenty-two

years after its founding, there were 2814 conferences, including, besides those in Europe, thirty in the United States, nineteen in Mexico, thirty-five in Canada, and a number in Asia and Africa. And the work of Ozanam and his friends has proved to be just as enduring and fruitful in the twentieth century.

The rapid spread of the Society was more amazing because it was received with some suspicion in certain quarters, especially by the civil authorities and by older Catholics. In part this mistrust grew out of the innate conservatism of nineteenth-century French Catholics who feared anything new. Ozanam, in a letter to Lallier written in 1838, describes with unaccustomed sarcasm the opposition to the Society in Lyon. "It is not possible to have any illusions, the Society has encountered opposition everywhere. . . . It has never ceased to be an object of mistrust to many of the laity." He goes on to caricature bitterly those who attack the Society: "big shots of orthodoxy, heads of councils in frock coats and long trousers; doctors who deliver their condemnations between the reading of the newspapers and discussion about business, between the peas and the cheese; people for whom the new is always bad, for whom everything coming from Paris is presumed to be perverted."

Opposition was not restricted to Lyon nor to elderly laymen, for in Paris difficulties were also encountered. The clergy there were by no means entirely hostile, and Ozanam testified in Lyon to the support of many "venerable priests," but there was misunderstanding and doubt, arising largely from confusion as to the aims and nature of the Society. Thus in 1838 a representative of the archbishop of Paris attended a meeting of the Paris conference. Although the Society had been in existence for over five years with reports of the meetings sent to the ecclesiastical authorities, the representative of the archbishop did not expect to find an active, effective organization. In the pithy words of Lallier: "They imagined that they were dealing with thirty or so jokers meeting in order to deliver speeches to each other."

Yet another cause of misunderstanding, if also of strength, was the exclusively lay character of the Society. In the years immediately subsequent to its formation, when the direction that the Society was to take remained uncertain, when its rules of procedure and organization were in the process of development, the possibility that it would pass under the control of the clergy was real. Ozanam was determined that it should remain as it had been at its commencement, entirely under the direction of the layman. In one of his letters to Lallier in which he made fundamental recommendations as to how the development of the Society should proceed, Ozanam wrote as follows:

> The power of presiding over the meeting should be exercised, not by the pastor, but by the president of the Society. The minutes should express it in these terms, "reverend father honored the meeting by his presence." A meeting place should be found, if possible to avoid the inconvenience of meeting in the Church.

Such insistence upon lay control of the Society, particularly when it is remembered that it was not, as it often is today, a question of control by older important members of the parish, but rather of young students, was doubtless the cause of much suspicion among the clergy. Anticlericalism was a popular sport in nineteenth-century France, so that the stubborn determination of the leaders of the St. Vincent de Paul Society to resist clerical domination must have appeared to many as another manifestation of this practice.

Furthermore some ecclesiastical and lay authorities discerned in the Society liberal even revolutionary tendencies.

Nothing gives a better picture of the almost paranoic fear of nineteenth-century Catholic rulers than this mistrust of the St. Vincent de Paul Society. To accuse an organization such as this of not only sectarian political activity but of attempting to undermine legitimate governments verges on the farcical. Yet such was the case! As late as 1852 the Society was banned in the Grand Duchy of Tuscany because of its alleged connection with liberalism. It was only after Ozanam, at this time in Italy because of his health, explained in a private interview with the Grand Duchess the purpose of the Society that the ban was lifted. On several occasions other than this, Ozanam testified that one of the obstacles to the extension of the Society was the vague fear that under veil of charity there was a political end. For this reason the leaders of the organization made every effort to divorce it from all political connections; all Catholics were welcome to join, no matter what their political philosophy or position.

Despite the opposition, the mistrust, the misunderstandings that surrounded the early years of the St. Vincent de Paul Society, it was an immediate success; indeed, it grew with a rapidity that is almost incredible. In purely human terms, this is difficult to explain; the temptation is to appeal to a superhuman power, to describe it with Ozanam as "a providential fact." Still some attempt at a more natural explanation must be made. To do so, let us examine the nature and aims of the Society in order to gain some insight into the hearts and minds of the thousands of young Catholics who were attracted to it.

Perhaps nothing stands out more about the St. Vincent de Paul Society, in the overall picture of the nineteenth-century Church, than its positive character. The Church of the past century, especially in France, was largely on the defensive. In the midst of an increasingly secular, un-Christian

world, Catholics and the Church reacted chiefly in a negative manner: opposition to the threatening dangers was the
motif of much Catholic activity.

It is true that the primary factor in the foundation of the
St. Vincent de Paul Society was the anti-Christian atmosphere in which these Catholic students found themselves.
But Ozanam and his friends refused to respond to this
danger in a purely negative fashion, for their aim was to
put into practice the truths of Christianity, to seek Christian
answers to the dangers and difficulties facing the world.

Ozanam, in a speech delivered near the end of his life,
described the circumstances behind the first meeting of the
Society. He pictures himself and his friends living in a
heterodox world insofar as religion and philosophy were concerned. Surrounded by many and conflicting systems and
ideologies, these young Christians felt the necessity of meeting together to strengthen their common faith. Furthermore,
they desired to give an example of their faith, to live publicly
that which they believed. They sought to answer the criticism
that Catholics were contributing nothing to the improvement of their society, that Christianity was out of date.
Specifically, according to Ozanam, they were responding to
a challenge made to them by fellow students, followers of
the doctrines of the Utopian Socialists, Saint-Simon and
Fourier. These devotees of the new social religions charged
that Catholicism was dead and its works sterile. In the words
of Ozanam:

> they said to us: "You are right if you speak of the past: chris-
> tianity has in other times performed prodigies; but today chris-
> tianity is dead. And, indeed, you who boast of being Catholic,
> what do you do? Where are the works which demonstrate
> your faith and which will make us respect and acknowledge it?"

The St. Vincent de Paul Society was formed to provide

the answer to this indictment, to provide the works that would demonstrate the vital character of their faith and the example that would lead their non-Christian fellow students to respect them and their religion, and perhaps, in some cases, to join them in it. It was not founded to combat socialism, liberalism, Protestantism, atheism, or any other opponent of the Church, but to permit its members to exercise charity toward others in the community, especially toward those most in need. It was organized so that its members could be living witnesses of Christianity within their society. Here, surely, is a major reason for its popularity.

Another explanation for the appeal of the St. Vincent de Paul Society to nineteenth-century Catholics is its lay nature. Today the position and importance of the layman in the Church has become increasingly magnified, but this was not the case in the first half of the nineteenth century. The Church then was still under the influence of the largely rural, stable society of preindustrial Europe. In these conditions the parish was the center of community life, while the priest, often the only educated person, was much more than just a spiritual leader. All this was breaking down in the changing world of the nineteenth century. The life and actions of Ozanam himself — that he, a layman, could exercise such an important influence upon the Church — was a symptom of this. But many of the clergy did not understand the change that was taking place, and they resented the attempts of the laity to exercise leadership in the Church. The opinion expressed by a prominent English monsignor who was close to Pope Pius IX represented the view of many of the clergy. "What is the province of the laity?" asked Monsignor Talbot, according to the latest biographer of Cardinal Newman. "To hunt, to shoot, to entertain. These matters they understand, but to meddle in ecclesiastical matters they have no right at all." With persons holding such opinions occupying important positions in the Church, the opportunity for independent lay action was limited. The St. Vincent de Paul Society, without in any way being anti-clerical, provided an opportunity for such action. Little wonder that it appealed to zealous, energetic nineteenth-century Catholics.

A third, and major, reason for the attraction of the St. Vincent de Paul Society was its work with the poor. It is true that the primary aim was not simply the amelioration of the life of the poor, for the assistance given to the indigent was a means to an end, not an end in itself. The end sought was to improve the spiritual life of the members of the Society through the opportunity to exercise the virtue of charity. Hence the St. Vincent de Paul Society was not, in any sense, a social reform movement. That the aid given to the poor was not exclusively material is a proof of this, for the spiritual as well as the material occupied the attention of the Vincentians. Members of the Society concerned themselves with, among other things, the task of returning Catholics to the practice of their faith, with domestic difficulties, with the development of habits of prayer. Educational work was likewise undertaken: books were passed out, adult study groups organized, and lectures delivered. Ozanam and the Lyon conference, for instance, busied themselves with the soldiers of the Lyon garrison in an effort to improve their education.

Despite the fundamental spiritual end of the St. Vincent de Paul Society, despite its lack of concern with the root causes of modern poverty, the work of the Society with the poor was a magnet that drew many bourgeois Catholics to it. This is so for two reasons: one, the enormity and the immediacy of the problem of social justice; two, the failure of the upper classes and the Catholic Church to offer any viable answers to the problem. Under these conditions, the efforts of the St. Vincent de Paul Society, feeble and peripheral though they may have been, were at least an opportunity for Catholics to act in this crucial area.

To appreciate fully the significance of the charitable work of the Society it will be necessary to digress from the main theme in order to describe in some detail the socioeconomic conditions of the France of Ozanam's day. Actually this journey into the wasteland of the misery and privations of the urban poor is not a side trip, since the issue of social justice, which Ozanam on several occasions referred to as the most interesting and important question of the age, was, to change the metaphor, interwoven throughout the fabric of Ozanam's life.

It was not simply a matter of poverty and suffering among the lower classes, for behind this immediate, day-by-day struggle over wages, living conditions, and the necessities of life, a cataclysmic, irresistible movement was under way. A new, industrial, mass society was being born. Its birth pangs were violent, turning away many sincere, concerned, upper-class Catholics in fear and disgust. Not so Ozanam! His concern for justice was not blighted by the radical means that were sometimes used to try to achieve it. His understanding of the obligations of the Christian to act in the issue of social justice was not clouded by the turmoil and violence that accompanied the struggles of the urban poor to improve their lot.

Statistics as to the privations of the poor during this period are easily obtainable. In one department in the north of France, where industrialization was more general than elsewhere in the nation, one sixth of the population was on relief. In 1836 in Paris, it has been estimated that there were 30,500 men who had no regular work and another 50,000 entirely unemployed. An economic survey of the day summed up the situation of the urban poor as follows:

> When work is continual, the salary average, [and] the price of bread moderate, a family could live with a sort of ease and even make some savings if there are no children. If there is one, it is difficult, impossible if there are two or three. Then it can survive only with the assistance of the government or some private charity.

Nor was it simply a matter of low wages and long hours of work, since living conditions in these rapidly growing cities were terrible. Slum is too weak a word to describe the hovels in which the working class often lived. Some made their homes in caves; whole families resided in a single room; the better off slept on straw mattresses, the others on dirt floors. Naturally, violence, disease, and immorality were endemic in such conditions; cholera, tuberculosis, alcoholism, and prostitution gorged themselves upon the body of the urban poor. The debilitating effects of all of this upon the health of the workers is shown by government statistics; for example, the percentage of those turned down for military service was twice as high in the industrial areas as in the rest of France. One contemporary report estimated the life-span of the child of the factory owner at twenty years while the average life-span of the child of the worker in the factory was seventeen to nineteen months!

Cold statistics fail to give life to this tragic picture. Let us read the description of a visitor to the homes of the poor of Paris. It was a family tradition of the Ozanams to visit the poor, with both of Frederic's parents practicing the virtue of charity in this way, and very likely, as a child, Frederic had accompanied them. As an adult, and as an active member of the St. Vincent de Paul Society, Ozanam continued to visit the poor throughout his life. Hence the lines that follow are, in popular phraseology, an eyewitness account. The place is Paris, the time 1848:

Half of these districts [the workers' section of Paris] . . . are made up of narrow, twisting streets where the sun never penetrates, where a carriage cannot move without danger, where a man in a dress coat cannot pass without causing excitement and bringing to the doors groups of naked children and women in rags. On both sides of a foul gutter stand some five story houses, several of which contain fifty families. The lower rooms, because they are damp and loathsome, are rented at one franc, fifty centimes, when they have a fire-place, and one franc, twenty-five centimes without it. They are without wall paper, often without furniture to hide the bareness of their walls. In a house on the rue de Lyonnais, which is known to us, ten families no longer have any beds. At the back in a sort of cave lives a family without any other bed than a little straw upon the bare earth, without any furniture than a rope which runs across the room; these poor people hang their bread in a linen rag in order to keep it away from the rats. In a nearby room, a woman has had three children die from consumption, and watches with despair three others destined for the same end. . . .

Let us not speak of those who have a better lot, who have two beds for six persons, where the sick and the well, boys of eighteen with girls of sixteen are crowded together pêle-mêle. Let us not speak of the raggedness of the clothes, which is such that in one house twenty children cannot go to school because of the lack of clothing. At least it is necessary that these unhappy people be given something to eat, so that if they perish of consumption, it will not be said that they literally died of hunger in the most civilized city on earth.

Granted that Ozanam's plea for the poor, for such it is, is not evidence of the general condition of the urban worker, still no one can gainsay that a serious problem existed.

Furthermore, the poverty and privations of the poor were made greater by the opulence and indifference of the upper classes. The government of France in the period 1830 to 1848 was the so-called July Monarchy of Louis-Philippe, a middle class, liberal government, with political rights restricted to the wealthy, and with an economic policy that was theoretically laissez-faire. In actuality, the implied impartiality and nonintervention of the government in disputes between employers and workers was a fiction, for the power of the State was used entirely to strengthen the position of the moneyed class. The attitude of the July Monarchy to the poor was expressed by Guizot, the leading minister of Louis-Philippe, when he answered the complaints of the poor against the privileges of the rich with these words, "Get rich yourselves."

The spirit of society was likewise hostile to the poor. The France of Ozanam's day was an increasingly commercial and industrial world in which the pursuit of wealth was the dominant motive. It is this bourgeoisie, materialistic society which is so bitterly and sharply drawn in the novels of Balzac. These masterpieces of literature are filled with speculators, misers, gamblers, and other types inflamed with the lust for money. In the real world of the July Monarchy the overpowering greed of the upper class left little room for concern for the unfortunate, for those who were unable to hold their own in this harsh economic struggle.

Faced with misery in the midst of opulence, with a government indifferent and even hostile to their interests, exploited by the prosperous upper class, the workers responded with a bitter hatred of society. Discontent, disturbances, and violence were common, with Ozanam's native city of Lyon the scene of some of the sharpest battles. In the years immediately following the Revolution of 1830 the silk workers of that city were often in the streets demonstrating against the conditions in which they lived and worked. In 1834 one of these street disturbances grew into a virtual civil war on a small scale as the silk workers and the army engaged in a battle of several days' duration in which artillery and other weapons of war were used against the rioters. Ozanam, on his return home from Paris for a school vacation, reported in a letter to a friend upon the evidences of battle visible in Lyon. The desperate situation of the workers is shown by a banner carried by them which read, "To live working or to die fighting."

That the charitable activities of the St. Vincent de Paul Society did not provide any solution to the problem of the urban poor is unquestionable. Christian charity could do little more than pick away at the edges of this desert of human misery that was the life of many of the lower class. The enormity of the problem dwarfed the good will and enthusiasm of these young Catholics. In 1840 Ozanam wrote that there were over 60,000 workers in Lyon demoralized. He reported that the Lyon conference was extremely busy endeavoring to assist these unfortunates, and yet its accomplishments must have been slight in this flood of misery. Solutions were needed, not stopgap, isolated efforts that prevented starvation but did nothing to eliminate abject want. Although it is just to criticize the failure of nineteenth-century Christians to realize that traditional charity, without an effort to root out the causes of poverty, was a mockery of the sufferings of the poor, nevertheless it is not fair to condemn the St. Vincent de Paul Society in this matter, since reform was not its intention.

In the case of Ozanam himself there is much more to be said concerning his approach to and understanding of the problem of social justice. Many Catholics, including intellectual leaders, did not understand what was happening, seeing only the need of controlling the violence and instability of the lower classes. Ozanam, however, had a clear grasp of the serious nature of the issue facing society. Ten years before Marx described in the *Communist Manifesto* the growing class war of industrial Europe, Ozanam had arrived at a similar conclusion. In a letter to his Vincentian friend, Lallier, he painted in lurid colors the conflict facing France:

> It is the battle of those who have nothing and those who have too much; it is the violent collision of opulence and poverty which makes the earth tremble under our feet.

For him it was egotism that was at the root of this class war. Particularly responsible was the individualistic selfishness of the rich, the "cult of myself," "the bad seed," which was constantly multiplying in society. Against this the workers paraded an egotism of their own that was principally a class thing, seeking to confiscate everything to its own interest. Between these two egotisms an irreconcilable hatred existed which could lead to a war of extermination.

This understanding of the class conflict that was developing did not lead Ozanam to any genuine solution for ending it. Since he had no particular training nor inclinations in the area of economics this should not surprise us. As a student he had attended the lectures of the Catholic economist, Charles de Coux, but de Coux, like most contemporary economists, was unable to suggest any new, viable program for the complex industrial world that was coming into being. His analysis of the faults of laissez-faire capitalism was intelligent, but on the cure of these faults de Coux had nothing of significance to say. It may be that Ozanam gained some technical information on the socioeconomic issues from de Coux's lectures, but he received little beyond this.

Insofar as Ozanam possessed a socioeconomic theory it was neither original or radical. Although he was strongly opposed to socialism, he suggested that there was a fruitful element in it, namely, the voluntary sacrifice of the individual to the needs of the group, which Ozanam held was essentially a Christian principle. "Society should be a consecration of each for the good of all and especially for the protection of the weak." From this it can be seen that Ozanam's social views were chiefly within the Catholic tradition. For him society consisted of various groups and organizations, what a modern political or social theorist would call corporations. The most basic of these was the family, upon which Ozanam would rest all other social forms, with the political community growing out of this. Since the individual required these groups in order to live the good life, he must contribute, by the voluntary sacrifice of his individual interest, to the good of the various corporations of which he was a member.

Ozanam's emphasis upon the community and upon the voluntary sacrifice of individual good for the good of the group placed him in opposition to the prevailing spirit of the July Monarchy. Laissez-faire economic theory, with self-interest as the motivating force in the life of society, was the commonly accepted view. To Ozanam this reliance upon self-interest to provide a satisfactory social environment was simply a rationalization of egotism and selfishness. Its effect, in his view, would be to reduce human life to the calculation of interest, to ruin the poor, and to close to them the sources of assistance which they need in order to live.

Yet, as we have mentioned, Ozanam was no socialist despite his rejection of laissez-faire capitalism. He accepted the principle of private property, provided the social obligations of wealth were not forgotten. He was also opposed to any forced government confiscation of property, sharing with most of his fellow Catholics of the day a suspicion of government intervention in these matters. Ozanam's economic theory, then, was that private property was a right and individual liberty a necessity; nevertheless, the voluntary sacrifice of a part of this right for the good of society was desirable, even imperative. Later in life, taught by the course of events, particularly the Revolution of 1848, he became more aware that private initiative and action were not enough, that leadership by the government was required, although his dislike of government action in this area never entirely disappeared.

The primary means by which Ozanam hoped to improve the life of the urban poor was the widespread practice of Christian charity. It was upon this virtue that he placed his chief hope for the future. Catholics, through the practice of charity, must mediate and reconcile the conflicting interests of the rich and the poor; this was an idea that constantly reoccurred in his correspondence in the years prior to the Revolution of 1848. Through their example, Catholics can, he hoped, persuade the rich to give up voluntarily some of their wealth and at the same time persuade the poor to accept with resignation their privations. Christian charity was the only means by which a catastrophe could be avoided. "God alone knows," he wrote, "what future awaits us, if Catholic charity does not intervene in time to stop this slave war at our very gates."

In retrospect it was naïve of Ozanam to expect such results from the practice of charity in the face of such a massive social problem, but his response was that of most French Catholics who concerned themselves at all with the lot of the urban poor. Faced with a new and fundamentally different problem, that of poverty in an urban, unstable, industrial society, these pious, generous Catholics relied upon the traditional methods of aiding the poor, namely, through private charity.

As a result of this concern with charity the period of the July Monarchy saw a great increase in Catholic activity and organizations in this area. Ozanam and the St. Vincent de Paul Society were but a part of a wave of charitable work. The pioneer in this was a nun of the Order of St. Vincent de Paul, Sister Rosalie, whom we have already mentioned as the means by which Ozanam and his friends were put in contact with the poor. Sister Rosalie had devoted her life to the poor of Paris. She and the members of her order lived in the working-class district where they established schools, orphanages, and other institutions. Her knowledge of the difficulties of these unfortunate people was intimate and personal, and she became the contact for Catholics who wished to engage in charitable activities.

Her most important convert to charitable work was an energetic nobleman by the name of Armand de Melun. When at the age of twenty-eight, de Melun, with the aid of Sister Rosalie, made a personal tour of the slums of Paris, he determined to devote his life to the effort of improving the lot of these people. His major contribution was that of founding and directing charitable enterprises, climaxing in the formation of an International Society of Charity.

Granted the limitations of such an approach, still in fairness to these zealous Christians it must be reiterated that they had no guidelines to follow. The enormous problem of social justice for the working class was only beginning to unfold itself. Officially the Church neither made any statement upon it nor advanced any social program until the social encyclicals of Leo XIII appeared much later in the century. It is to the credit of those who sought to serve the poor that they recognized the problem and attempted to deal with it, albeit unsuccessfully.

In this they differed from the majority of French Catholics who either ignored their obligations or shared the prevailing laissez-faire, self-interest view of the issue. These Catholics justified their failure to act by a number of rationalizations, such as the threat to order and property contained in the discontent and disturbances of the working class. They suggested that any effort by the government to interfere in the area of poverty was an infringement upon the rights of the Church, which had traditionally dealt with this social evil. For example, when de Melun advanced the idea of some welfare legislation, the conservative Catholic newspaper, *L'Univers*, attacked him with the charge that he sought to put the State in place of the Church.

Nor can it be said that the charitable work of the period of the July Monarchy was entirely a failure, for it bore fruit in an increased sympathy for the Church among the urban workers, the group which had been most disaffected toward Christianity. The February Revolution of 1848, when churches and priests were respected by the revolutionists, as contrasted to the hatred and violence shown to them in 1830, is evidence of a reconciliation of the Church and the workers. Tragically, later developments of 1848 and the years that followed destroyed the gains of the previous year.

Furthermore, the charitable activity of these Catholic organizations may have served to develop a social conscience in many upper-class Frenchmen. It is difficult for us to realize the chasm that existed between the life of the poor and the well-to-do in French society. Armand de Melun illustrates this. Born and raised in provincial France of a prominent and wealthy family he, like Ozanam, came to Paris for his education. It was not, however, until his twenty-eighth year that this sophisticated, cultured nobleman obtained a personal knowledge of the misery and sufferings that were the life of many of his fellow citizens. He had lived completely sheltered from this. He has described for us his feelings as he first crossed into the working-class district of Paris. It was, he wrote, as if he were entering a new, strange land; his reactions were a combination of curiosity, amazement, and fear.

Certainly all active members of the St. Vincent de Paul Society had the opportunity to see for themselves the life of the poor, for it was a basic rule of the Society that the members must personally visit those they were assisting. Hence, very possibly, Ozanam and his Society may have made an important contribution to the development of a social conscience among upper-class French Catholics.

A further defense of Ozanam's reliance upon private charity as the means of overcoming the evil of urban poverty is his exalted concept of this virtue. For him it could never be reduced to impersonal philanthropy which, as a sop to conscience, gives alms to the poor. In an early letter he distinguished between this and charity:

> Philanthropy is a pride for which good actions are a kind of finery and which loves to look at itself in the mirror. Charity is a tender mother who keeps her eyes fixed upon the child that she carries in her arms, who no longer thinks about herself and who forgets her beauty in her love.

Charity, then, is love; it is a personal tie between those who give and those who receive. The alms given to the poor are meaningful only when they are given personally, with sympathy and interest for those who receive them. It is a truism of Christianity that the real beneficiary of charity is he who gives rather than he who receives: of this Ozanam was deeply aware, writing movingly and beautifully of it.

On one occasion he wrote of the spiritual advantages of aiding the poor in these words:

> Our faith is weak because we cannot see God. But we can see the poor, and we can put our finger in their wounds, and see the marks of the crown of thorns.

At another time he put it this way:

> They [the poor] suffer that which we cannot suffer, they are among us as messengers of God to test our justice and our charity, and to save us by our works.

Thus it was not impersonal philanthropy, nor occasional acts of charity to which Ozanam turned in the midst of the crisis facing his society; rather he sought a great outpouring of love. It is love that must warm the cold earth! In the past when society was sick, as in the thirteenth century, it was saved by "a vast effusion of love," such as that of St. Francis. It was precisely upon this that Ozanam placed his hopes.

If Ozanam's reliance upon charity as the method of ending the tragedy of the industrial poor was utopian, nevertheless such a spiritual, positive understanding of this virtue is most attractive. That he and his fellow Vincentians put this into practice makes it more appealing. Granted that the work of the Society did little or nothing to strike at the roots of the problem, still there was much value in their charitable activity. In purely material terms, it must have, in some manner, relieved temporarily the misery and suffering of a part of the poor. In spiritual terms, this "vast effusion of love" must have had incalculable results.

Chapter III Rejoice in the Lord

In 1836 Ozanam returned to his parental home in Lyon, having completed his studies at the University of Paris, although it still remained for him to finish his thesis. The four years at the university had been satisfying and full. The youthful Ozanam had used to the utmost his intellectual gifts and his religious zeal. The efforts of Ozanam and his friends to defend the Church in the hostile academic world of Paris had resulted in real and important achievements. At the same time, Ozanam had not neglected his studies; a measure of his success in this was that he earned degrees both in law and in literature.

The five years that followed, from 1836 until 1841, were neither as happy nor as rewarding as these student days, although they were crucial ones in his life. It was a period of sorrow and of stress, a period that tested and strengthened his faith; out of it emerged the mature Ozanam, settled in an academic career, with a deep understanding of the obligations of the intellectual Christian to his society.

Up to this point we have primarily been concerned with the outward, public manifestation of his Catholicism, appropriately enough since this is the subject of the book. But if we are to understand the mature Ozanam, if his efforts to relate his religion to his society are to be meaningful, the inward, personal aspects of his religious faith must be considered.

Here the historian faces certain problems. No one can ever measure the depth and content of the interior religious commitment of another. Very likely many do not understand their own internal assent to Christianity. Often it requires a great tragedy or a shocking experience before we become aware of the strength or weakness of our faith.

In some cases the biographer or historian is aided in his efforts to probe into the hidden, interior spiritual life of another by the writings of the individual involved. Many saintly persons, as a means of better understanding themselves, have put on paper their self-analysis, their interior meditations. Such sources are invaluable, but if Ozanam put his private thoughts on paper they have not been made public. Only in the two hundred or so letters that are a part of his published works can we obtain glimpses of his innermost private feelings. Unfortunately, in preparing Ozanam's letters for publication, the editors, in deference to the wishes of his family, eliminated the most personal, the very ones that would have been the most useful to those who wished to know this side of Ozanam's life.

But there are other methods and sources available to us. Certainly it is permissible for the historian to assume, if there is no evidence to the contrary, that the life of an individual will have an overall consistency and coherence. In other words, we can safely assume that the outward devotion and dedication to Christianity which dominates Ozanam's public life and actions are a reflection of a deep, living, inward commitment to that faith. Surely it can be taken for granted that a life which in its outward aspect was wholly directed by Christian principles must rest upon strong spiritual foundations.

We have also the testimony of many who knew him intimately, all of whom write in glowing terms of his religious zeal, of his charity and piety. Some of them, notably the Dominican Lacordaire and Ozanam's older brother, Alphonse, also a priest, write of his private spiritual exercises. They write of his daily prayer, of his frequent reception of the sacraments, of the fact that Ozanam regularly read the Bible for a half hour each morning. Lacordaire describes his simple, austere life: for example, flowers, which he loved to have about him, were Ozanam's greatest personal luxury.

The biographical memoir of his brother, Alphonse, is especially useful to us because of what it can tell us of Frederic's efforts at self-improvement. For instance, the friends of Frederic's mature years stress his kindness, his affectionate, pleasant nature. Yet his brother tells us that as a boy Ozanam was often irascible and short-tempered. Thus the pleasant, amiable adult was not the product of a natural disposition but rather of the will and discipline imposed on the man by himself. Likewise Ozanam had a strong strain of melancholy in his personality; throughout his life he had to fight against a temptation to discouragement and dejection. Still his writings, particularly after 1840, display an intellectual trust in Providence which enables Ozanam to face the world in a posture of courageous optimism. Naturally the will and the intellect can never entirely overcome a tendency to sadness, to despondency, but the dominant reaction of Ozanam to life is optimistic, this despite his own poor health and the dangers of serious social crisis. Once again it is the triumph of his faith over his natural predilections.

But the crucial test of religious faith comes in times of trouble, for it is in such periods that the strength and weakness of a religious commitment appear. For Ozanam the years following his return from Paris, from 1836 to 1840, were just such a time. In 1837 his father had an accident which proved fatal. Not only did Ozanam sorely miss the love and protection of his pious father, which he described as the human equivalent of Providence, but besides heavy family responsibilities fell on the twenty-four-year-old youth. His older brother's duties as a priest took him away from Lyon for most of the time, while his younger brother was still in school. And it was at this time that the health of his mother began to fail. For three years Ozanam watched as death gradually stole his mother's life, surely a harsh experience for any son. Eventually her mind was affected, and the young man could no longer turn to his beloved mother for consolation and advice. Finally, in late 1839, she died, and although her condition was such that her death was expected, Ozanam was desolated. As he wrote to a friend "what havoc this death has made in my heart." Characteristically he added, "Happy the man to whom God has given a holy mother."

The depth of his sorrow over the death of his mother and the consolations that religion gave him were brought out eleven years later when a friend suffered a similar loss. Ozanam wrote a letter of sympathy in which he told of the sorrow that he still felt. "She has left you," he wrote, "and I know all the bitterness there is in this thought, since it draws tears from me in recalling that eleven years ago, my mother left me also. No, this wound will never close; time will not dry your tears, God will give you other consolations; but in the midst of your most beautiful days, you will remember suddenly all that you have lost, and your eyes will fill with tears."

Thus does Ozanam picture the human, natural sorrow of a son who has lost a beloved mother; but for the Christian, he tells his bereaved friend, there are spiritual balms to heal the ache. Death does not separate the members of a family, for the dead watch over and intercede for those still on earth. Here is how Ozanam expressed this thought:

> It is not only a memory which remains for us, it is not only the hope of having as protectress with God her who was our guardian here on earth: it is the certitude of being still in close communication with her; it is the feeling of her presence around us, and the warmth of her wings which has not ceased from covering us. Sometimes when I am in difficulty, suddenly and when I least expect it, I believe I hear this voice which gives me courage! Sometimes also, in a day of joy and success, it seems to me that she comes to take part in it and rejoices to see us happy! I cannot treat this as an illusion; it is something too animated and too penetrating, which tells me that my good mother lives still with me.

The difficulties and sadness of these years were intensified by the financial obligations which he now had to assume. He was the support of his younger brother and his sick mother, which meant that he had to practice law, a profession for which he had little liking. Although he received some pleasure from his oratorical success in the courtroom, for the most part he found the work unsatisfying. He was too much of a theorist, too much of an idealist to enjoy the compromises and negotiations which make up a lawyer's life: in his words, "discussions over pecuniary interests are painful to me." Perhaps the greatest cause of his dislike of law as a profession was that it kept him from his first love: literature. Indeed, the melancholy that pervaded these years was, aside from his family tragedies, largely the result of his longing to return to the academic world, to the intellectual life of the university.

That Ozanam was depressed and restless during these years arose in part from the needle of youthful ambition. It was surely difficult, after the triumphs of his student days, with the inner knowledge of his intellectual talents, to turn his back on the academic world. It seemed that life was passing him by, that he was stagnating in dull, provincial Lyon, far away from the intellectual, exciting world of Paris. He described his situation this way: "I have learned the science of abnegation which is always difficult for me. Is it vanity that makes me think I have more to do than practice law in Lyon?"

Although his evaluation of his talents was realistic, still there was in his attitude in these years an immaturity and a worldly ambition that did not come up to either his profundity or his spirituality. This youthful superficiality with regard to the earthly duties of a Christian was shown in a letter he wrote to Lallier in which he criticized severely the latter's intention to marry and settle down in provincial France. Ozanam's disgust with this was shown by a biting question that he asked: "Is it not suicide when a person such as you goes to Sens to plant cabbage?"

It was, however, only human for the young, enthusiastic Ozanam to wish to achieve success in the profession that he loved. Furthermore, as always, his strong religious foundations overcame his natural propensities. Despite his melancholy, despite his strictures upon the dull, prosaic life of a provincial lawyer, Ozanam could still pray to God, "that I may be resigned to do His Will, whatever the humble role, whatever the sorrowful mission, that He has prepared for me. But let this will be known to me."

As the last sentence indicates, Ozanam was faced with another perplexing problem, namely, whether he had a priestly vocation. This would be a difficult decision under

the best of circumstances; in the midst of a family tragedy
it was especially so. The issue came to a head when in 1838
his friend from his Paris days, Père Lacordaire, left for Rome
to join the Dominican Order. It was Lacordaire's intention to
restore the Dominicans to France, from which they had been
banned. It was at this time, while Lacordaire was in Rome,
that he invited Ozanam to join with him in the task of bringing back to France the Order of St. Dominic.

The invitation came at the very moment when the crisis
of his mother's illness was reached, so that no immediate
decision was possible. Ozanam, however, was deeply troubled
over his future and seriously considered accepting Lacordaire's
offer. He wrote to the latter in August, 1839, on the question of his vocation as follows:

> It is this interior evil [his indecisiveness as to his vocation]
> from which I have suffered for a long time, for which I ask
> your charitable prayers; for if God wants to call me to him,
> I do not see any better troop in which to serve him than that
> in which you are engaged.

But his uncertainty continued. He wrote to his cousin some
months later that he "walks day by day by the road that
Providence leads me without seeing its end." The death of
his mother found him still in doubt as to what his decision
would be. It was his intention to await developments in the
hope that Providence would inform him as to what he
should do.

In such a fundamental matter Ozanam did not sit passively
waiting for inspiration, nor did he rely on human expedients.
He wrote to several friends that they should pray that he
receive the grace to make the right decision. Meanwhile, he
himself intended "by more religious life, by more austere
habits, to acquire some right to a light from on high, some
control over passion here below, [and] by this to have some

certitude of acting under legitimate inspiration." And eventually Providence did guide him, for in 1840 the question of both his career and his marriage was settled.

The years from 1836 until 1840 were then for Ozanam difficult and troubled ones. The loss of his parents, dissatisfaction and boredom over his personal and professional situation, and the perplexity as to his future vocation, all of this placed a heavy strain upon the young man. With his propensity to melancholy, it is not surprising that he often gave way to morbid thoughts and feelings. His letters to his friends of his student days are full of discontent and sadness. In them he broods over the tragic end of his happy parental home; he puzzles over what his future will be, and he eagerly asks of the news of Paris while complaining over the dullness of his life in Lyon. Even his prayers and spiritual meditations are affected, for he mourns the aridity of his spiritual life and wonders "why do I not find the repose that others find before the crucifix?"

Yet he does not give way to despair nor to inactivity, for his faith is too strong, his mind too healthy, too sane for this. He seeks, as we have seen, by prayer and self-discipline the grace to know his vocation. It is in this troubled period of his life that the melancholy, restless Ozanam contributes so greatly to the work of the St. Vincent de Paul Society. In brief, his depression, his discontents, his worldly ambitions are surface manifestations of his personality. Underneath this anxious, somewhat immature appearance was a deep, vital spirituality that permitted the youthful Ozanam to face with serenity, even with joy, the privations and sorrows of life. Read, for example, the letter he wrote in 1837, at the age of twenty-four, in the midst of personal difficulties. It goes in part as follows:

You see life does not appear to me a bed of roses. . . . I will tell you, in order to keep nothing back, that the blackest images have shown themselves to me. A little more than a week ago the prolonged contemplation of my interior and exterior miseries so overcame my spirit, that I was at the point where it was impossible to think or to act. My head was on fire, drawn to all kinds of desolating thoughts, and the most desolating of all was perhaps my own state. This extreme sickness caused me to turn to the doctor, to the doctor, I mean to say, who has the secret for moral infirmities and who has the deposit of the balm of divine grace. However, after I described, with an enthusiasm uncommon to me, my sorrows and the causes of my sadness to this charitable man that I call my father, how do you think he answered me. He answered by these words of the Apostle: *Gaudete in Domino semper!* Isn't this a strange statement? Here is a poor man who has the greatest unhappiness in spiritual things, that of offending God; the greatest unhappiness in the order of things of nature, that he sees removed by absence or death several friends to whom he was tenderly tied. . . . He is still more in anguish over an uncertain future, crushed by cares and tasks the best of which wound him; if he retires within himself in order to flee from the distressing situation outside, he finds himself full of weaknesses, imperfections, and faults; and the humiliations and the secret sufferings that he causes himself are not the least painful. And he is told, not to resign himself, not to console himself, but to rejoice: *Gaudete semper!* It requires indeed all the audacity, all the pious insolence of Christianity to speak in this way. And yet Christianity is right.

The year 1840 saw a break in the clouds that darkened Ozanam's life, for in that year the two most fundamental decisions of a young man's life — those of his vocation and his marriage — were settled in a most satisfactory manner.

Throughout the years since his return from Paris, Ozanam had yearned to go back to the academic world. Unfortunately his family circumstances, the necessity of providing for his ailing mother and his younger brother kept him in

Lyon where he engaged in the practice of the law, a profession he had chosen only to satisfy his father. His professional situation improved somewhat when the city of Lyon, proud of the reputation of the young scholar, created a special chair of commercial law for him. Then, late in 1839, Ozanam's mother died, and it was at this very moment, when the filial ties binding him to Lyon had been removed, that an opportunity to realize the dream of his life, an academic career in the field of history and literature, was offered to him.

The instrument by which this new path was opened to Ozanam was a former professor of his at the University of Paris, Victor Cousin. Although he is virtually forgotten today, Cousin was at that time one of France's most illustrious scholars. He had been greatly impressed with the brilliance and eloquence of Ozanam when the latter was a student at the university. So greatly did Cousin value the talents of Ozanam that he became determined to bring the young man "into his regiment," to attract Ozanam away from law and into an academic career. The interest that Cousin showed in Ozanam in 1840 was continued throughout the latter's life, to the great advantage of Ozanam. Over the years the two men came to a mutual esteem and respect, although they were never intimate friends. Since Cousin's philosophic position was not Christian, his patronage of a Catholic scholar such as Ozanam, in the midst of a society in which religious controversy raged, is a credit to his open-mindedness.

In 1840 Cousin was the National Minister of Public Education. Under his sponsorship the University of Paris proposed to offer a competitive examination in the field of foreign literature, with the winner being given an opportunity to join the faculty of the university. Cousin wrote to Ozanam to suggest that he take part in the competition.

Several factors made it appear that Ozanam would have small chance of success. The areas of knowledge upon which the candidates were to be tested were extensive; Classical and French literature, fluency in several foreign languages, and a knowledge of several European national literatures were among the fields to be covered. Since the prize was so alluring, the top young scholars of France would naturally be attracted. At the same time, Ozanam was committed to lectures on commercial law and needed a considerable amount of time for their preparation. Likewise the circumstances of his mother's death as well as his indecisiveness in deciding to accept Cousin's offer to enter the competition meant that he would have much less time for preparation for it. Cousin himself did not think that Ozanam had any chance of finishing first because of these reasons. Nevertheless, in part because of the friendly pressure of Cousin, who did believe that Ozanam would add to the brilliance of the competition, in part because this was opportunity, albeit a remote one, to return to those studies which were the breath of life to him, Ozanam decided to make the attempt.

Feverishly, he set to work. Always an exceptionally hard worker, Ozanam now put in fifteen and more hours a day of study. In a few months' time he reviewed the major literature of Europe as Homer, Plato, Dante, Shakespeare, Racine, Schiller, one after the other were studied. So rapidly did he pass through the ranks of these illustrious figures that, so he wrote, they were like phantoms to him.

Finally the day of the examination arrived. Seven candidates presented themselves, among them several professors of Classical literature. After the first day, in which he had to prepare a paper in Latin upon Roman tragedies and an essay in French upon Bossuet's funeral orations, Ozanam was so discouraged that he would have quit had not one of the judges indicated that he had done well. The competition continued in Classical and French literature as well as four modern ones, concluding, after a week of examination, with a speech delivered by each candidate upon a topic drawn by lot. Ozanam drew the "History of the Greek and Latin Scoliasts" as the subject upon which he had to speak. He was overwhelmed by the esoteric nature of the topic upon which he knew little or nothing. Indeed, the audience (for the competition was public) laughed when the title was read, for it seemed a hopeless, even absurd topic. Charitably given some assistance by another candidate, Ozanam spent the night in preparation. The next day he spoke for almost two hours to the applause of the audience and, much to his astonishment, was placed first in the competition. Consequently, in the following year, he joined the faculty of the University of Paris as an assistant to the professor of Foreign Literature, M. Fauriel.

His triumph was a genuine *tour-de-force* because his educational background and experience were not equal to those of most of the other candidates. His victory resulted from his boundless energy, his strong memory, and his natural talent for eloquence, attributes which were to make him an outstanding teacher and lecturer.

Clearly Ozanam was extraordinary in his intellectual gifts; this, combined with a great enthusiasm for truth and persistent industry, gave him great potential as a scholar. This was recognized by his contemporaries, for in 1844 at the very youthful age of thirty-one Ozanam was appointed to the Chair of Foreign Literature at the University of Paris. At this time the university was the first academic institution of France; indeed, its position was so elevated that it had no rivals. Its faculty included many of the leading scholars of the nation, so that membership in this intellectual elite was the pinnacle of academic success.

Despite his early attainment to the summit of the profession, despite his great potential, Ozanam's contribution to scholarship is not outstanding. For thirteen years he lectured and wrote on the literature of the Middle Ages, but his premature death in 1853, at the age of forty, cut him off at the height of his powers. Forty, in a profession in which maturity comes late, is only the commencement of a career. Had Cardinal Newman, for example, died at this age, all of his great works would have remained unwritten. Still Ozanam's published works run to ten volumes, containing aside from private letters and his writings on contemporary issues, a genuine contribution to medieval historiography. These historical works are, however, only the groundwork, an outline of what might have been. Had Ozanam lived to complete his survey of medieval literature, he might well have earned a permanent, exalted rank among historical scholars. As it is, his historical writings are today largely of value only as historical curiosities.

The year 1840 was decisive in the life of Ozanam for yet another reason, for in December of that year Ozanam wrote to Lallier to inform him of his engagement to Amelie Soulacroix. At the end of the academic year of 1841, the first for Ozanam as a lecturer at the University of Paris, he and Amelie were married. This gentle, cultured girl (she was not yet twenty-one) was the daughter of the rector of the academy of Lyon. The family background of the two young people was similar: both came from Catholic, professional, even intellectual, middle-class families. The twelve years of their marriage were very happy, especially when, in 1845, a daughter, Marie, was born to them.

Under these circumstances it is amusing to read a letter that Ozanam wrote in 1835, at the age of twenty-two, in which the young bachelor expressed his dislike of the marital state. His objections are typical of an immature young man who has spent his life in a chiefly masculine atmosphere. For example, he could not understand how anyone could give up his independence to live with another, nor how two persons could live in such intimate circumstances, especially when one was an irrational, emotional woman. As late as 1839, less than two years before his marriage, Ozanam repeats to Lallier his criticisms of the marriage state. He writes of it as "this double egotism," as an abdication of the dignity of a man. Needless to say, this misogamy is entirely forgotten two years later.

Behind the youthful Ozanam's strictures on marriage was the assumption that it was for him, in some sense, an inferior state. In his letters to Lallier, Ozanam described virginity as "the most beautiful flower that can be cultivated in the garden of the Church." Regardless of the truth of this statement, and regardless of the relative merits of marriage and the celibate life, Ozanam obviously needed family life. Psychologically, and therefore spiritually, he was much healthier after his marriage. In the years before this event his letters show him to be despondent and unhappy. It is true that this was a difficult time for him, with the problem of choosing a vocation and the death of his parents weighing upon him, still his despondency was probably in part the result of an unconscious dissatisfaction with the single state. Although Ozanam had, as we have seen, a strong character and an attractive personality, he shared the fate of the sons of Adam in that all was not perfect with him, as his strong tendency toward melancholy, against which he had to struggle all of his life, shows. Perhaps because of this element of temperament, Ozanam could not bear to be alone too much but enjoyed having people around him. The benefits of a happy family life to such a temperament are obvious. Furthermore, a nature as generous as his needed someone to whom he could give himself. He recognized this need within himself, but in the years before 1840 he could not decide whether the priestly vocation should be the means of satisfying it. As he wrote: "I sense in myself a great emptiness which neither friendship nor study can fill: I do not know what will come to fill it: will it be God? will it be a creature?"

Later in life Ozanam came to appreciate the spiritual advantages of family life, particularly the habit of sacrifice which marriage developed. Thus when he attempted to draw up a social theory, he stressed that sacrifice was necessary for society; the family, he insisted, was the school in which individuals learned to make the sacrifices for others which society required.

Marriage, then, for Ozanam was not an inferior, negative element in his life, but a positive, fruitful factor in his spiritual and intellectual growth. Clearly his temperament and his mind flourished in the midst of a happy home life. And the deep religious strength upon which he drew in the last years of life when personal and public tragedy darkened his existence owed much to his two "earthly guardian angels," as he called his wife and daughter.

Thus ended upon a happy note a difficult and troubled period in Ozanam's life, one in which his religious faith was refined in the furnace of personal sorrow while his uncertainties as to his future vocation had made him more aware of himself and his potentialities. Out of these years emerged a more mature and wiser man, one prepared to carry out the duties of the Christian intellectual in the new academic career upon which he was now entering.

Chapter IV The Sword of the Modern Age

In later years Ozanam referred to his student days as "his golden years," and the accomplishments of these young men, of whom Ozanam was the leader, are impressive. At the same time, his glorification of his youth does not do justice to his maturity, for it is to the last fifteen years of his life, especially after he entered upon his academic career in 1841, that we must turn to witness the full development of his Christian attitude toward the modern world. Of great interest, and the subject of this chapter, is Ozanam's understanding of the duties of the Christian intellectual in a pluralistic society.

In 1841 Ozanam and his bride moved to Paris to take up residence, making their home there, aside from travels for his health, until his death twelve years later. Throughout this period he remained associated with the University of Paris, lecturing and writing on the subject of medieval literature. He was most successful in his academic career, although cut off in the full flower of it. As we noted above, he reached the pinnacle of academic success when he was appointed in 1844 to the Chair of Foreign Literature at the

University of Paris. Both his lectures and his historical writings were well received by contemporary scholars. He was chosen for membership in several international academic organizations, while he himself had some hope of election to the *Academie Française*, the recognized intellectual and literary elite of France. His early death put an end to any possibility that he might some day realize this hope.

The achievements of his scholarly career are much more impressive when its abbreviated nature is remembered. In a sense, his professional life had just commenced when he was afflicted with a fatal illness. He personally lamented the abortive character of his scholarship in a letter written a few months before his death. In it he pointed out that he had only succeded in laying the foundations of his historical scholarship, grieving that he would never have the opportunity to build upon these foundations.

Doubtless Ozanam was ambitious to succeed in his career, doubtless he relished his scholarly triumphs. Thus in 1841, on the occasion of his first lecture at the Sorbonne, Ozanam shared with his fiancée, in a letter to her, his fear of failure as well as his joy over its favorable reception. He described in detail the response of the audience to this or that point, dwelling with evident satisfaction on the compliments he had received. His concern for the favorable development of his career was also shown by his reaction to his appointment to the Chair of Foreign Literature. Upon the death of the holder of the chair, Fauriel, there was some question as to whether Ozanam, who had served as his assistant and substitute, should be appointed. Actually the post was offered to J. J. Ampere, who refused it. This period of uncertainty and waiting as to the final decision upon his appointment weighed heavily upon Ozanam. His love of teaching and of scholarship, as well as the imperative necessity of supporting his family, brought him to a high state of anxiety and agitation over his future. As always in matters of personal concern, he feared the worse. He wrote in letters to friends very pessimistically over his future in the academic world, contemplating bleakly his youth, his lack of an established reputation, and his Catholicism as factors that would prevent his appointment.

When after weeks of waiting his appointment was made public, Ozanam was overjoyed. Certainly his motives for rejoicing over his permanent appointment to the faculty of the University of Paris were legitimate — security for his family, an independent and dignified position, final certainty as to vocation in work that he loved — nevertheless the pious Ozanam felt "ashamed to be so moved by a temporal success," as he wrote to Ampere. To another friend, Foisset, he went on in the same vein: "There is something dishonorable for a Christian to be touched so deeply by a temporal advantage."

It was not scrupulousness nor a false spirituality that led Ozanam to mistrust his happiness over his professional success, but rather a concept of the mission of the Catholic lay intellectual. It was not enough, believed Ozanam, for a Christian to use his mind and talents to make money or to achieve worldly recognition, for the "lay" intellectual — using the term "lay" to indicate those working in nontheological studies — must dedicate himself and his scholarship to the service of God and his faith. This is, for Ozanam, the primary justification for such a vocation.

From his youth Ozanam had made just such a dedication. As early as the age of fifteen he had decided that he would endeavor to spend his life in historical studies, the goal of which would be the glorification of Catholicism. His uncertainty as to his career — whether it would be religious, law, or academic — did not affect this fundamental decision. No matter where his choice might fall, it was his intention to use his intellectual gifts for the defense and the promulgation of his religion. For example, if he had eventually settled upon the legal profession, it was his aim to prepare a work on the beneficial influence of Christianity upon the development of French law.

This dedication of his mind to the cause of Catholicism did not mean that Ozanam was simply a polemist, simply a writer of partisan tracts. Next to religion his love of truth was the dominant force in his life. In his mind there was no contradiction between the dedication of the mind to Christianity and the search for truth, because for Ozanam, as for St. Augustine, all truth is one. Hence natural knowledge, what Ozanam calls science, must necessarily lead to God and must serve to glorify Him. All truth, no matter how trivial, no matter how widely divorced from religion, will ultimately lead to the source of truth, i.e., God.

This then was, in Ozanam's mind, the goal of the Christian lay intellectual: to seek truth in the various nontheological areas of study, for the truths discovered in these sciences will necessarily glorify God and defend religion. No better example of the attainment of this goal can be found than the historical writings of Ozanam himself, for in this he is the personification of his thought.

The goal of seeking truth in science, in the area of natural knowledge, imposes other duties on the Christian intellectual: specifically, he must work and study so that he can master the techniques and details of whatever field of knowledge he has chosen. Ozanam constantly stresses the obligation all men have to labor, for work is "the law of regeneration" that all men must follow. "Useless servants of God we may be," he wrote on one occasion. "Lazy ones never."

For the intellectual the duty to work is doubly pressing, since it is only through patient, arduous research that the scholar can gain the knowledge and the training necessary to find truth.

Once again Ozanam is the personification of his thought. He gave of himself wholly in the service of truth and the defense of his religion. He wrote extensively in the periodical press on contemporary issues and during the Revolution of 1848 was an editor on a Catholic newspaper. He spoke often to various Catholic, worker, and intellectual associations, and was for years the director of an adult study group which met regularly in Paris. He was active in the Society for the Propagation of the Faith and served it with his pen. To the end of his life he worked tirelessly for the St. Vincent de Paul Society, serving as president of the Lyon conference and as vice-president of that of Paris after he moved to that city. In his travels he missed no opportunity to speak and to proselyte for the Society; for example, at the very end of his life, although he was so weak from illness that he could scarcely stand, he delivered speeches to the newly formed conferences of Florence and Leghorn.

All of this was aside from his academic work, which was the chief occupation of his life. Both as a student and as a professor, Ozanam labored diligently in the pursuit of knowledge. His power of work was amazing, and he constantly drove himself to the limit. As a student he worked regularly twelve hours a day and, so he wrote to his younger brother, Charles, to encourage him in his studies, for several months in preparation for an important examination he averaged fifteen hours a day. This incessant industry and study continued after his appointment to the faculty of the Sorbonne. It was not uncommon, especially in the first years of teaching, for him to stay up very late preparing for the next day so that he came to the lecture room so exhausted that he could hardly complete the lecture. At times his weariness was so evident that friends advised him to work less, not to seek every source and citation possible to support his statements. Vacations, even those caused by ill health, did not halt this constant study. In 1846, for example, Ozanam had a serious illness and was advised to take a year off from teaching in order that he might travel and relax. His friends, aware that he could not rest without some useful task to occupy a part of his time, arranged with the Ministry of Education that he be given the job of searching the libraries and archives of Italy for historical documents. Hence the fruit of this vacation for his health was the publication of a volume of documents upon medieval history.

The depth of his feelings upon this as well as the limits to which he pushed the obligation of the Christian intellectual to work and study was demonstrated when in 1847, in a speech delivered to a Catholic group in Paris, he lamented that he did not work harder, this at the very time when, still weakened by illness, he was lecturing, writing, and working almost continually. In the same speech Ozanam compared the obligation of the Christian intellectual to give himself wholly to his work to the life of the missionary; both are asked to give up their lives to the cause of Christianity, the missionary in far-off lands, the intellectual in the study and the lecture room. In this, as in his understanding of the other duties of the Christian intellectual, Ozanam's life exemplifies his thought. He was anything but a lazy servant of God, for he labored long and hard in the vineyard of his Lord.

The results of this labor were a great fund of erudition and a close acquaintance with the literary sources of medieval history. Ozanam's historical writings consistently show a wide range of knowledge with a constant citation of evidence and fact to support the argument. This can be found in the first serious product of his pen, an essay against the Saint-Simonian socialists, written when he was eighteen. It can be found in a much stronger and general form in the last and most mature of his historical works, *Civilization in the Fifth Century*, published after his death. Here the years of dogged research are evident in Ozanam's familiarity with the sources of the period. If it is the duty of the lay intellectual to master the area of study that is his, a perusal of Ozanam's writings will show that he had lived up to a high degree to this obligation.

Thus far the duties of the Christian lay intellectual vocation as viewed by Ozanam — the dedication of his mind to God and his religion, the obligation to search for truth, the duty to work and to become competent in his area of study — have no exclusive application to the modern world, for they hold true for the Christian scholar in any society. But there is one duty that rests heavily upon the shoulders of the Christian intellectual in a pluralist society, such as that of nineteenth-century France: that is, the obligation to engage in controversy. Religious controversy, for Ozanam, has nothing odious about it so long as it is conducted in a charitable manner, for open discussion is a legitimate means of defending and promulgating religious truth. If the freedom of man and the voluntary assent to belief are to be respected, force can have no place; therefore, debate, carried on in an open, charitable fashion, remains an important means of convincing nonbelievers of the truth of Christianity. This duty of engaging in Christian controversy necessarily falls chiefly upon the lay intellectual because the arena must be that of natural knowledge, since the non-Christian usually knows nothing of and is uninterested in theology. Consequently, it is doubly imperative in the modern world that the Christian pursue truth in the nontheological studies, for, writes Ozanam, "the sword of the modern age is knowledge."

The battlefield upon which Ozanam wielded this sword was history; the basic theme running through his writings was the beneficial effects of Christianity upon the development of civilization. In the words of Ampere, Ozanam's work shows "Christianity glorified by history."

Ozanam's interest in the relationship between history and and Christianity was a product of the culture in which he lived. Romanticism, the predominant cultural trend of the day, was essentially historical in its thought; for example, the origin and development of institutions, cultures, and ideas were problems which attracted the Romantic mind. Philosophy of history (the attempt to systemize and to synthesize all history) was of widespread interest, with such thinkers as Hegel and Comte, among others, attempting to master this problem. Christian thinkers were deeply affected by this stress upon history; indeed, the strongest argument for the truth of Christianity to many Romantics was the so-called traditionalist one. Briefly, the traditionalist argument ran something like this. All societies and civilizations can be shown to have possessed a religion, hence religion is natural to man. Of these various world religions, Christianity can be shown to be the most reasonable and the most useful in improving man and society. It is, therefore, the true and natural religion for mankind.

Although this proof, if proof it be, has little appeal to the twentieth-century mind, it was a basic weapon in the Christian Romantic's armory. Ozanam, a Romantic through and through, accepted and used it; so strongly did he rely upon it that it is no exaggeration to say that it forms the very basis of his historical thought and writings. At the early age of fifteen he had already determined that the demonstration of the truth of Christianity by history would be his lifework. At that time, with the boundless enthusiasm of youth, he entitled his future work: "Demonstration of the Truth of the Catholic Religion by the Antiquity of its Historical, Religious, and Moral Beliefs," a title whose awkwardness is matched only by its ambiguity. Not surprisingly, this great, if vague project was never realized, but Ozanam remained true to his youthful purpose, if on a more limited and realistic scale. He also remained convinced, until the end of his life, of the strength of the traditionalist argument as a proof of the truth of Christianity. Thus, a year or so before his death, in answer to a letter from a friend of his student days who had since lost his religious faith, Ozanam suggested that he turn to the study of history in order to find the evidence and proof necessary for him to regain his Catholicism.

By his choice of history as the ground upon which he was to fight, Ozanam chose to besiege the major citadel of the French anticlericals. In his eyes, the anti-Catholic movement in France was the child of Voltaire; "All irreligion in France," he wrote, "still follows Voltaire. . . ." In this he was joined by his liberal Catholic friend, Montalembert, who divided Frenchmen into two families: the sons of the Crusades and the sons of Voltaire.

The opposition of Voltaire and his fellow eighteenth-century *philosophers* to the Catholic Church was largely based upon its evil historical influence. Most of these French anticlericals, although themselves not religious, believed that religion was necessary for society. The truth or falsity of a religion was not the point, since for them, all revealed, supernatural religions were unprovable, but rather the social, mundane effects of religion were the crucial issue. For them the power and influence of the Catholic Church upon history was entirely malign, for it bred ignorance, intolerance, and darkness. Those periods of history in which the position of the Church was dominant were necessarily eras of retrogression; thus, the thousand years from the fall of the Roman Empire to the Renaissance of the fifteenth century, the middle ages between two great cultures, were unworthy of the attention of scholars, for it was simply an age of superstition and barbarism, a truly dark age.

It was this attack that Ozanam was determined to answer. It was not to be polemics nor theology but, as required in Christian controversy, a genuine historical answer to an attack based upon history. He was convinced that, for the most part, this view of the Catholic Middle Ages as the Dark Age was false; as he wrote, "I do not know if Voltaire has a greater enemy than history."

Because of his premature death Ozanam's finished work is largely restricted to the transition period when the Roman Empire was disintegrating while medieval culture developed, the period referred to by modern historians as the Early Middle Ages. Here Ozanam ran head on into another of the giants of eighteenth-century historiography, Edward Gibbon. Gibbon, and those who shared his philosophic and humanistic outlook, treated this period from the point of view of classical culture, as the collapse of the great civilization that was Rome. For them this was an entirely catastrophic event which led to a great cultural regression. So deep was the abyss into which Western Europe plunged in the fifth century that it took over a thousand years for that society to climb laboriously and slowly back to the cultural heights of the Roman period.

All of this is true enough if the events of the fifth century are viewed only from the point of view of Roman civilization, and it must be realized that in historical writing the point of view of the historian is crucial. Ozanam, however, chose to look at these happenings not as the end of a civilization but as a fruitful period in which the seeds of a new culture were laid: namely, that of the High Middle Ages, and through it modern Western civilization. Since the Catholic Church was the dominant institution in the Europe of the Early Middle Ages, this interpretation necessarily led to a stress upon the positive contributions of Christianity to Western civilization.

Ozanam did not limit himself to vague generalities as to what these contributions were. He pointed to the theology and philosophy of the Church Fathers, particularly that of St. Augustine and St. Jerome, as the means by which much of classical thought was passed on by the medieval Church to modern culture. Nor was the contribution of the Church limited to the negative task of preservation, for the dogma and institutions of the Catholic Church in the centuries immediately subsequent to the fall of the Roman Empire effected such basic changes in society that a new culture was formed, one that proved to be, once it reached its full development, not inferior to the Roman Empire. In other words, argued Ozanam, the fall of Rome was not, in the long run a retrogressive event, but a progressive one.

Some of the specific effects of Christianity upon culture brought out in Ozanam's writings are: it weakened slavery, which was at the basis of Roman culture; it improved the status of women; it stressed the importance of the individual; and it dignified labor. Modern liberty, often considered the antithesis of medieval Christianity, owes much to the developments of that age. In a word, Ozanam was one of the first students of the fifth century to make the point that twentieth-century historians stress: that the Catholic Church in the centuries following the fall of Rome brought about a psychological revolution. The fundamental attitude of Western man to the world and to life was basically altered, and a new society, the seedbed of the modern world, was planted.

This briefly is Ozanam's interpretation of the Early Middle Ages. It is admittedly a Catholic view, for Ozanam was consciously defending his religion against an historical view that was hostile to it. Granted this, it nevertheless remains good history. To appreciate this, the interpretative element in historical truth must be understood. All historians have a bias, a point of view, when they examine the past, especially when they deal with issues and questions that are of current interest. What is demanded of the historian is that he strive to find the truth, that he search for it in the records of the past, and that he base his conclusions upon the evidence found in these records. If he honestly does these things, his presentation of a past event or period will possess an objective validity. As we have already seen, Ozanam was a thorough and precise researcher, an assiduous student of historical sources, who constantly cited evidence for his views. Obviously Ozanam felt strongly the responsibility of the historian to adhere to the rules of his science, while his confidence that truth will ultimately serve Christianity gave him no reason to fear the result of honest historical research and writing.

Apparently there were those among his contemporaries who felt that he was too Catholic in his scholarship, because at one time he took the trouble to defend himself against this charge. In his defense he made no effort to deny that he wrote for a cause, that of defending his religion, but he also insisted that he did not do so at the cost of truth. He wrote in part on this point:

Two things only may be demanded from an author. Firstly, that his belief shall be independent and intelligent, and Christianity requires not less. Secondly, that the desire to justify a conclusion shall not induce him to distort facts in order to produce the desired proof. . . . They [Christian writers] know that it is not permissible to deny any truth, however profane, however embarrassing. They make it a point of conscience not to hide any stain which dims the lustre of any glory. If their research succeeds in justifying revealed dogma, they state the fact and rejoice for love of truth. If it be not given to them to remove obstacles, and to lead science to the point of union with faith, they know that others will press on. They are patient for they know that, though the way is long, God is at the end.

Ozanam's historical presentation of the Middle Ages lives up to these rules. Although he stressed the positive elements in that culture — as a good Romantic he was much attracted to it, calling the Middle Ages his "enchanted island" — he did not hide its flaws. For example, in the introduction to his *Civilization in the Fifth Century* he wrote of the danger of too great an admiration by Catholics for the Middle Ages. The historian must not, warns Ozanam, in his praise of the glories of this Catholic culture, ignore "the horror of constant wars, the brutality of feudal institutions, the scandals of these kings always in battle with the Holy See."

Proof of the genuine scholarship of Ozanam's historical writings is the reception that they received from contemporary scholars. As was noted above, he, as well as his books, were honored not only by Catholic associations and groups but by various secular organizations. Furthermore, it must be remembered that Ozanam lectured and taught in a university controlled by a government that had a strong tinge of anticlericalism in it. Pure polemics or Catholic apologetics would have soon brought an end to his connection with such an institution.

How well have his historical works stood the test of time? In all honesty it must be admitted that they have been almost forgotten, except by the specialist in historiography and French Romantic literature. Nevertheless, twentieth-century Medievalists have to a large extent come around to the view that the Early Ages is the period in which the roots of modern Western culture were laid. Whether they would follow Ozanam in all his conclusions may be doubted, but there can be no question that Ozanam's interpretation of the period is much more acceptable to historians of our day than Voltaire's picture of it as the Dark Ages.

The merit of Ozanam as a historian as well as the validity of his conclusions can be illustrated by a comparison of his work with that of a contemporary Catholic historian, Christopher Dawson. Although there is no evidence that the latter was in any way influenced by Ozanam, still their views of the Middle Ages are surprisingly similar. Both of them are avowedly Catholic in their history, but in each case it is a Catholic interpretation buttressed by deep erudition and scholarship. Both have a broad, cultural approach to history, relying strongly upon literary sources, with an emphasis upon the place of religion in society. Both see Christianity as one of the fundamental pillars of Western civilization, and the Middle Ages as a fruitful and significant period in the history of that civilization. So it is that Ozanam, despite the current obscurity of his historical writing, deserves to be placed among those great Romantic historians who pioneered the study of medieval history and who have had so many twentieth-century descendants.

The Catholic strain in Ozanam's scholarship is more understandable when the circumstances in which he lectured are known. He was associated with a secular university, under the control of the State, with a majority of colleagues who did not share his Catholicism. The hostility of many members of the faculty to the Church was increased by the attacks of Catholics upon the university. The motive behind these Catholic criticisms of the University of Paris was the monopoly enjoyed by that university in higher education in France. The leader of the Catholic crusade against this situation was Montalembert. With the support of even ultraconservative Catholics, Montalembert launched a vigorous crusade in favor of freedom of education, which in this context meant freedom for the Church to operate in the area of higher education. Montalembert also accused the university of causing young Catholics to lose their faith because of the anti-Christian sentiments of many of the faculty. In all of this Montalembert had the vociferous support of most of the Catholic press and leaders, including the extreme, polemical newspaper *L'Univers*. As a Catholic and at the same time as a member of the faculty of the university, Ozanam was placed in a difficult position. *L'Univers*, for instance, suggested that he resign, and when he did not follow its advice, criticized him as a deserter of the Catholic cause.

Ozanam bore all of this with restraint; he remained friendly with Montalembert and the Catholic opponents of the university monopoly as well as with his colleagues on the faculty. Doubtless a Catholic as sincere as Ozanam, who held strong views on the rights and freedom of the Church, was in general sympathy with the campaign conducted by Montalembert. On the other hand, he had obligations to his colleagues and to the university with which he was associated. Consequently, in his private letters, he sought, insofar as this was possible, to calm spirits and to avoid divisions both within the Church and within the university. For us, however, the interesting aspect of the situation is that it brings into sharp focus the unusual nature of Ozanam's professional position. The unique and difficult circumstances that he faced arose from the fact that the university with which he was connected was itself the center of a bitter controversy between Catholics and anticlericals in France. Inevitably Ozanam's Catholicism became an issue so that he personally was to some degree made a part of the whole controversy.

Yet another element in the university life of his day pushed Ozanam into the forefront of the religious struggle. This was that the lecture podium at a French university was often a platform from which a professor preached a particular ideology. The French lecture room lacked the calm, serene, withdrawn, if sometimes boring atmosphere of the American university, but was a place where current intellectual and political battles were waged. The lectures were open to the public, and often organized groups, both friendly and hostile, attended. The speakers did not hesitate to raise controversial issues which had no direct bearing on the subject that they were teaching, nor did the audience hesitate to show openly their approval or disapproval, sometimes in a rather violent manner.

Inevitably, under such circumstances, academic lectures became an accepted weapon in the bitter struggle raging between French Catholics and anticlericals. Often the issue was present only by implication, in that a professor might become a symbol of a particular party, so that the partisanship of the audience would be made known no matter how innocuous the lecture; such was the situation in 1844 with a Catholic colleague of Ozanam's, Lenormant. On occasions, however, the lecture room became the focal point of the struggle, as was the case in 1843–1844 at the height of the fight over the University of Paris.

The disturbances and tumult that troubled the academic scene at this time began not at the university where there were few extremists from either side but at another institution, the *College de France*. Both sides bear a responsibility for the series of incidents that occurred. It began when two of France's most famous scholars, Edgar Quinet and Jules Michelet, both republicans and anticlericals, concerned over the Catholic campaign against the university, decided to use their positions at the *College de France* to attack the Church. Quinet, for example, digressed from the official subject of his lectures, the literature of Provence, to deliver an attack upon the Jesuits. In these discourses Quinet attempted to demonstrate that the Church, and especially the Jesuits, were hostile to freedom and to the spirit of modern France. Indeed, argued Quinet, the Catholic Church in modern times was opposed to the very spirit of Christianity itself. To replace this repressive and evil Church, Quinet offered a new, secular religion of humanity, with the people as its god, republicanism as its dogma, the Jesuits as its devils, and Michelet and Quinet as its prophets.

The next year, 1844, Quinet now found that lectures upon ultramontanism were necessary for an understanding of the literature of Provence, while Michelet, the foremost historian of France, preached similar sermons in his lectures on history.

Nor were Catholics without sin in all of this. It was, indeed, the bitter and, in Ozanam's eyes, unjustified attacks on academic lectures by Catholics that provoked Quinet and Michelet. Furthermore, organized groups of Catholics, with Veuillot of *L'Univers* as the instigator, invaded the lecture rooms of the *College de France* in an effort to prevent anticlerical professors from speaking. Boos, hisses, catcalls, and a general uproar were the methods used to achieve this end, and the first of Quinet's lectures on the Jesuits was delivered to the accompaniment of pandemonium. As might be expected, anticlerical students and groups responded in kind. The victim in this case was Ozanam's colleague at the University of Paris, Lenormant. Although he was not an aggressive, polemical personality, Lenormant had made the mistake of explaining to his audience how his studies had brought him to become a Catholic. In 1844, he became the symbol of Catholicism at the university, the victim of an organized campaign to disrupt his lectures. The situation became so bad that Ozanam, to indicate his support for his Catholic associate, attended his friend's lectures. On one occasion Ozanam became so upset by the systematic clamor in the room that he leaped to his feet to make a plea for fairness and justice to the speaker. Since the government of Louis-Philippe would do nothing to insure order in the lecture room, Lenormant was eventually forced to give up, and to resign his position at the university.

Such were the circumstances under which Ozanam wrote and lectured. No matter what his personal inclinations may have been (and he was not by nature a polemist), he was pushed to the forefront of the controversy by his position as a lecturer at the University of Paris. When all of this is kept in mind, the Catholic element in his scholarship does not seem excessive. At times, it is true, such as in 1843, Ozanam delivered lectures directly aimed at answering attacks against the Church, but in general his writings and lectures were not polemical but scholarly. The proof of this is that he retained the respect and friendship of his non-Catholic associates on the faculty as well as by the absence of demonstrations against his lectures.

Nor were Ozanam's intellectual battles restricted to jousts with French anticlericals, for some of his most bitter duels were with fellow Catholics over the posture that the Church should assume toward the modern world. Thus it was that Ozanam found himself continually involved in controversy. Once again, in his use of his intellect in the defense of Catholicism, Ozanam is the personification of his concept of the Christian lay intellectual.

But in his stress upon the obligation of the Christian intellectual to engage in controversy, Ozanam also emphasized that it must be done in a Christian manner. Christian controversy forbids anger, resentment, extreme and violent arguments. The Christian intellectual should always remember, he points out, that the aim of controversy is not to smash or to humiliate those who disagree, but to convince and to attract them. He warns, in words that were directed to the Catholic polemist of his day but which apply equally to the controversialist throughout the history of the Church from Tertullian to twentieth-century extremists, that too often "the holiness of the cause has been compromised by the violence of the methods used."

Ozanam's rejection of polemical, violent methods in debate was a product of both temperament and conviction. His was an open, generous nature to whom the practice of charity to others was fundamental. At the same time, he was intellectually convinced that progress in spreading truth could only be achieved by free discussion conducted in a courteous, charitable manner. In 1846, when the controversy over the State monopoly in higher education was still alive, he wrote to Lallier of his personal approach to religious debate. The Catholic cause, asserted Ozanam, can be served by two methods of controversy: that of war and polemics and that of peace and charity. Whatever may be the advantage of the more violent approach, for him proselytizing by charity was to be the only means.

His preference for courteous, scholarly discussion in matters of religion rather than for polemical, bitter argument shines through all of his writings. Rarely does he use sarcasm and irony, never personal invective, and this includes not only his public writings but his personal, private letters. In the entire ten volumes of his collected works there is not a single personal attack upon a contemporary opponent, surely a remarkable record considering the extent of Ozanam's personal involvement as well as the intensity of the struggle.

The best example of Ozanam's fulfilling the duty of Christian controversy can be found in his activity as a lecturer at the University of Paris. Here was Ozanam, a Catholic, addressing an audience composed of many who did not share his religious faith. And before his mind was the specter of the fate of his friend, Lenormant, forced from the University of Paris by the disruption of his lectures by anti-Catholic demonstrators. Neither of these circumstances prevented Ozanam from defending Catholicism by his interpretation of medieval history. But he did so in such a manner that he did not anger those who disagreed with him; rather they were attracted to him personally and, in some cases, to his ideas as well. His influence upon students in making them receptive to Christianity is incalculable, but there can be no doubt that it was great. After his lectures he was usually surrounded by a crowd of people who wished to speak to him privately. Students stopped him in the halls of the Sorbonne and in the streets of Paris; many came to see him at his home, where the door was always open to them. On at least one occasion, he received a letter informing him that one of his listeners had returned to the practice of his religion through Ozanam's lecture, an event that must have been repeated many times, granted the appeal of Ozanam's scholarship and personality.

Doubtless the careful preparation and the amassing of evidence in part explains the success of his lectures, but Ozanam was also blessed with great natural eloquence. In the words of his friend J. J. Ampere, he "prepared his lectures like [they were] a benediction and delivered [them] like an orator." Ozanam was that rare creature: the erudite, precise, industrious scholar with a gift for words. Whether writing or speaking, he was a stylist of the first order, clear and orderly in his presentation, able to improvise glowing, effective metaphors, especially in the heat of a lecture, to light up otherwise dry material.

His success as a Christian controversialist was also in part a result of his personality and character. His love of truth, his sincerity, and his enthusiasm attracted all who heard him. His sympathy for others, as well as his desire to reach his listeners, made him sharply conscious of their reaction and spurred him to seek to interest and to attract them. Along with all of this, his natural timidity and diffidence were an added appeal. His modesty was such that only when he was carried away by his subject and by his enthusiasm did he forget himself enough to attain true eloquence. But all who heard him agree that once this point was reached, Ozanam was superb. No better testimony of his success in Christian controversy, of his ability to appeal to those who did not agree with him can be found than the words of Ernest Renan, a noted foe of Catholicism, who wrote, "Ozanam we love you. What a beautiful soul!"

Chapter V The Cross at the Threshold of the Modern World

Ozanam's exercise of the duty of the Christian intellectual was not restricted to his academic career, nor to his Catholic view of medieval history. He also engaged in controversy in the defense and promulgation of his religion over contemporary issues and battles. It was in these struggles that he developed his liberal Catholic attitude toward the modern world. Fundamentally this liberalism was not political, as the name might indicate, but rather a question of the attitude that the Church and the individual Catholic should take toward their society: namely, the need for a reconciliation between the Church and the modern world.

His liberal Catholicism should be seen as a part of the controversy over this matter within the French Church. In the period from 1830 to 1848, while Louis-Philippe was on the throne of France, the battle lines between the so-called liberal and conservative Catholics were drawn, and a struggle that was to continue into the twentieth century commenced. Although the conflict on the surface was largely over political issues — the question of the legitimate Bourbon monarchy

79

predominated — behind this outward manifestation was the more basic question of the position of the Christian toward nineteenth-century France. Ozanam saw clearly that this was the key to the division among French Catholics. Here is how he described the conflict:

> There are two schools that seek to serve God through their pen. The one seeks the most radical paradoxes, the most debatable thesis, whatever will irritate the modern spirit. It presents the truth not by the approach which attracts but by that which repells. It does not seek to bring unbelievers back but to stir up the passions of believers. . . . The other school has for its end to seek in the human heart all the secret cords that can attract it to Christianity, to reawaken in it the love of truth, the good, and the beautiful, and to show that the ideal of these things to which the human heart aspires is found in revelation; to bring back finally the strayed and to increase the number of Christians.

To Ozanam, then, the conservatives on the whole rejected and condemned the "modern" world, while the liberals stood for a reconciliation of the Church and the new society of the nineteenth century.

An example of the rejection of modern society is the journalist, Louis Veuillot. This gifted writer, a product of the slums of Paris, was staunchly opposed to the innovations of his century. His hatred for the developments of the age is demonstrated by his hostility to such apparently innocuous changes as the railroad, the steamship, the telegraph, and urban renewal. These, for Veuillot, were the work of the devil! It is a sufficient commentary upon the official position of the Church in the nineteenth century to note that Pius IX approved and supported much of what Veuillot wrote.

While Veuillot and his associates were entrenching themselves in these extreme positions, the liberal Catholic movement was taking root. In fact it was just at the moment that the young Ozanam first arrived in Paris in 1831 that the first significant attempt to reconcile the Church to modern France began. This was the movement centering around the Abbé Lamennais and the journal, *L'Avenir*. Lamennais was an unusual and talented writer, whose rhetorical, literary style appealed to the Romantic taste of the day, and whose enthusiasm and sincerity attracted to him a group of able young men devoted to the liberal cause and to its leader. Of these young men, Count Montalembert and the priest, Lacordaire, were to be the most important. The attitude of the group is indicated by the title of its newspaper, *L'Avenir* (*The Future*), in the pages of which Lamennais insisted that the Church should come to terms with the ideals of the French Revolution and the developments of nineteenth-century Europe. Unfortunately, after little more than a year of publication, *L'Avenir* was condemned by Pope Gregory XVI. Although the Pope did not censure either Lamennais himself nor the principles for which he stood, but rather the excesses in language and thought in *L'Avenir*, Lamennais tragically refused to accept the decision of the Pope and left the Church. His defection deprived the liberals of an outstanding leader (granted that he was somewhat unstable and extreme), but the movement continued with Montalembert and Lacordaire as its foremost figures.

Soon after his arrival in Paris, Ozanam became acquainted with both of these men and remained friendly with them until his death. It was especially Lacordaire who influenced and cooperated with Ozanam in his liberalism. From the period of his arrival in Paris until his death Ozanam was heart and soul devoted to the liberal Catholic movement. His historical studies convinced him that the Church had to adjust to the modern world just as his enthusiasm and zeal brought him to a more positive outlook toward his society. With such views and with his ardent temperament, Ozanam was drawn into the thick of the battle between two Catholic groups. And battle it was, bitter and vitriolic, between brothers of the same faith: like all civil wars, war to the knife.

The conservative Catholics, possibly because of the defensive nature of their position, were particularly extreme and personal in their arguments, and of them, Louis Veuillot was the most partisan and poisonous. Despite his personal piety, Veuillot was consistently intemperate and unjust in his writings; he distorted, exaggerated, and argued *ad hominem*. From his position as editor of the conservative Catholic periodical, *L'Univers*, Veuillot launched his venomous barbs at those he considered to be the enemies of the Church. On several occasions Ozanam was the victim of these attacks. Veuillot accused Ozanam, among other things, of holding un-Catholic political and social views, of defending heresy, and of deserting the Catholic cause by his association with the University of Paris.

None of this caused Ozanam to modify his position in any way, while he remained, as always, moderate and temperate in controversy. He wrote in the midst of these acid, internecine battles that it was good for the Church to have several parties and points of view representing her interests, each serving the causes of the Church in its particular fashion. The closest that Ozanam came to a personal attack upon the conservative Catholics was when, in a private letter, he wrote of "the lost children of *L'Univers*, whose intemperance and lack of talent weakened their influence."

Despite Ozanam's personal friendship with Montalembert and Lacordaire, it was not these men who were the chief intellectual ancestors of his liberalism. This honor belongs to two literary figures of the Romantic movement, Ballanche and Chateaubriand. This is further evidence that Ozanam's liberalism was not primarily political, for neither of these men was an important political personality, at least not at the period that Ozanam knew them, while Chateaubriand was actually conservative in his political philosophy. Instead it was their desire for a reconciliation between the Church and the modern world that places them in the camp of the liberal Catholics, and it is this which attracts Ozanam to them. For him they are the true fathers of the liberal Catholic movement, for it is they "who have planted the cross at the threshold of our age."

Of these two men Chateaubriand was by far the more important historical and literary figure, but it is Ballanche who most influenced Ozanam. When Ozanam first arrived in Paris, Ballanche was an elderly man with some reputation as a writer and a philosopher, best known for his intimate friendship with the great Chateaubriand. Ballanche was a native of Lyon and a friend of Andre Ampere, with whom Ozanam lived in his first years in Paris. Doubtless it was these circumstances that help to explain his great influence upon the mind of Ozanam.

In an obituary written shortly after the death of Ballanche, Ozanam stressed the personal example he gave to young Catholics living in an anti-Christian world, but it was in the realm of ideas that the influence of the older man is most apparent. In his writings Ballanche sought to demonstrate the material benefits of Christianity to civilization. He emphasized social evolution and change to such an extent that he was accused of holding the evolution of Christianity itself. Optimism, in regard to both present and future, characterized his thought; a new age, a renewal was, in Ballanche's opinion, about to occur, with Catholicism having a significant role to play in it. Furthermore, this new age was to be one of democracy and of technology, in which the masses and the machine would be essential elements. Progress, democracy, and the mundane benefits of Christianity are thus at the basis of Ballanche's social philosophy, just as they are at the basis of Ozanam's.

Ozanam's liberal Catholicism, then, was not fundamentally a matter of politics; nevertheless, then and now, many observers considered the movement as a whole essentially political. And, it is true, some of the leaders were chiefly political liberals, with no genuine desire to reconcile the Church and modern society. Montalembert, perhaps the best known nineteenth-century French Catholic liberal, is a case in point. This aristocratic, rather arrogant intellectual was an ardent defender of liberty for the Church and for individuals, but he felt only repugnance for the mass, democratic society that was being born. He wrote to his close friend, Lacordaire, on this as follows: "I do not in the least admit your principle, that in order to influence one's age it is necessary to hold it in esteem." Whatever may be the abstract truth in this statement, the historian, looking back more than a century, can only say that such an attitude has produced disastrous results for the Church in the modern world.

A further reason for the stress upon the political aspect of the liberal Catholic movement was that the struggle between the two camps of Catholics was largely over political issues. This is so because it was a political event, the French Revolution of 1789, that most deeply divided Frenchmen in the nineteenth century. In general, French Catholics were in opposition to the influence and ideals of this event, while the secular, republican, liberal elements, who personified the new and the modern in French society, supported it. Thus the division of nineteenth-century France was accomplished with the French Church on the side of the Old Regime, pre-1789 France.

The hostility and hatred of French conservative Catholics for the French Revolution was expressed most eloquently and persuasively by an Italian nobleman, Count Joseph De-Maistre, whose writings became a sacred text to French royalists on into the twentieth century. For this reactionary aristocrat, the ideals of the French Revolution — the rights of man, written constitutions, representative government, and equality — were not only fallacious and anarchial, but also immoral and evil. DeMaistre, a pious Catholic, considered the Revolution as demonic; it was a providential event, in which God loosed the forces of evil to punish the French people for their sins. It was God's intention, at least according to DeMaistre, that the French nation through its sufferings should be brought back to the truth. Consequently, it was the duty of Catholics to oppose the influence of this evil event and by overcoming it to return France to the path of righteousness.

It was the rejection of the French Revolution to which the liberal Catholics, including Ozanam, reacted. If a reconciliation of the Church to modern society was to take place, Catholics would have to accept the legitimate conquests of the French Revolution. This was the basis of Ozanam's political position. His attack upon the conservatives was two-pronged: on the one hand, he sought to separate the Church from the monarchy, to break once and for always the union of the throne and altar; on the other, to demonstrate that the fundamental ideals of the French Revolution, especially that of liberty, could be reconciled to Catholicism. Hence, although Ozanam's liberal Catholicism was neither in its origin nor its basis political, since he sought primarily a reconciliation of the Church to modern society, nevertheless, the means by which he hoped to attain this end fell within the political sphere.

Ozanam was in no sense a political doctrinaire, for he did not insist upon any political system as an absolute. He would support, so he wrote, any government that exercised a legitimate authority and that permitted liberty, leaving it to circumstance to dictate which system would operate most successfully. For example, Ozanam always maintained that in the abstract he was a monarchist, yet in the world of the nineteenth century, democracy appeared to him to be the most workable and acceptable system.

Up to this point, omitting his acceptance of democracy, Ozanam's position was generally that of the liberal Catholics. But in his awareness of the mass, popular nature of modern society, he leaves the mainstream of the movement. Indeed, his advocacy of democracy places this moderate, gentle, scholarly man among the radicals of nineteenth-century French Catholics. Most upper-class Catholics of that day, including those with liberal leanings, feared and mistrusted the increasing power of the lower classes. For them the democratic movement was a threat to liberty and property, not the achievement of self-government and self-help by the masses. The two foremost nineteenth-century liberal Catholics, Montalembert and the English nobleman, Lord Acton, for instance, never reconciled themselves to the democratic movement. Ozanam, and those who worked with him, particularly Lacordaire, and in 1848, the Abbé Maret, in their grasp of the popular, mass, egalitarian nature of modern society, were far more perceptive than their better known fellow liberals. Ozanam can be placed beside his astute Catholic contemporary, Alexis de Tocqueville, in his conviction that the future is in the hands of the masses, for better or for worse.

Ozanam's primary objection to the royalism of the conservative Catholics was that they were tying the Church to an out-of-date institution, a bond which would necessarily injure Catholicism in France. He wrote, picturesquely enough, the following in this regard:

> I have without a doubt, all the respect for the old royalism that one owes to a glorious invalid; but I refuse to base my position upon it, because with its wooden leg it cannot march at the same speed as the new generation.

The fundamental error of the conservatives, according to Ozanam, was that they chained the Church, a divine, eternal institution, to the monarchy, a human, transitory system. These nineteenth-century Catholics, faced with a rapidly changing society, fell into the trap that has ensnared many twentieth-century Christians: viz., an inability to distinguish the essential and permanent in their faith from the circumstantial and the mutable. Many French royalists believed that the Church required the Old Regime and the legitimate Bourbon monarchy to fulfill its mission. This meant that the union of altar and throne became dogma, but it also meant, as Ozanam saw clearly, that the Church would be inextricably bound to a "glorious invalid." It was this that he strove to avoid.

In his desire to break the union of throne and altar Ozanam advocated the separation of Church and State. Since this was both a radical and a questionable position for a nineteenth-century French Catholic, some explanation of Ozanam's thought is necessary. It should be clear that he did not insist that the separation of these two institutions was abstractly and universally desirable, for he consistently maintained that in political matters, institutions and systems must vary with circumstances. As he viewed it, the Church could survive and prosper under any political system in which its rights were respected. The Church had no essential need of the State; hence the secular, areligious nature of the modern State did no harm to it. All that was required of the State, asserted Ozanam, was that it not prohibit what the Church ordains, nor ordain what the Church prohibits. Nor did he stop here, but went on to assert that in the modern world the Church actually benefits from separation from the State, pointing to the advantageous situation of Catholicism in Great Britain and the United States as evidence of his position. Once again, Ozanam was perceptive, even prophetic, in that the twentieth century has shown the truth in his argument; once again Ozanam's solution fits the needs of the Church in our modern, pluralist society.

Ozanam also argued that historically the separation of Church and State had made great contributions to Western civilization. Specifically, the struggle between the Papacy and the secular rulers of the Middle Ages permitted the development of modern liberty. Neither of these two institutions — Church or State — was able to gain dominance in both the religious and the civil sphere; hence neither possessed absolute control over the community and the individual. It was, in his view of the Middle Ages, the independence of the Church from the State that prevented the growth of absolute monarchy in medieval Europe.

Later in the nineteenth century, this particular argument concerning the medieval origin of modern liberty was developed in greater detail by Lord Acton. For us, however, the interest lies in the connection that Ozanam makes between Christianity and liberty. Liberty, the siren that has captured the hearts and minds of modern man, is, according to Ozanam, not alien to Catholicism, but a product of the historical influence of that religion.

Ozanam personally listened with love and veneration to

the siren song of liberty. It was the ideal of the French
Revolution which he stressed in his effort to reconcile the
Church and that event. Individual liberty for him, as for
so many other liberal Catholics, was an essential element
in man and the political community. Granted this indispens-
able quality of liberty, still Ozanam makes clear that he does
not mean by it a negative, absolute individualism. Typically,
it is the positive, social aspect of liberty which Ozanam
emphasizes, for he concentrates upon the limits placed on
liberty by law and upon the rights of others and the duties
of each.

Most significantly for Ozanam's goal of reconciling the
Church to the modern world, liberty, a major element in the
ideology of the French Revolution, can be shown to be
fundamentally Christian. Liberty, argues Ozanam, is the
power of acting spontaneously, which comes to us from God.
God is free because He is a law unto Himself, and He has
created man in His image. Human liberty, then, is analogous
to, and partakes of, the freedom of God; it is one of the ties
between the Creator and His creatures. Far from being opposed to Christianity, liberty is essential to it. It is, in
Ozanam's eyes, only in the centuries since the Reformation,
and particularly in the years since the French Revolution,
that Catholics have become foes of liberty. Liberal Catholics,
in their defense of liberty, are returning to an older and more
Christian position. Once the reconciliation of the Church
and liberty has been realized, asserts Ozanam optimistically,
the primary barrier separating Catholics from other Frenchmen will have been destroyed, and the Church will be able
to lead society to a new, more fruitful era.

This, briefly, is the argument advanced by Ozanam in his
effort to bring Catholics to accept the legitimate conquests
of the French Revolution, in his endeavor to have the Church

look with favor upon the political face of the modern world. But this is only one aspect of his liberalism; a second is his "social Catholicism."

The historian of French social Catholicism, J. Duroselle, has discerned two elements in the movement, both of which are to be found in Ozanam's thought: an awareness of the problem of justice for the working class and a belief in the possibility of social progress.

Ozanam, as we have seen in the discussion of the St. Vincent de Paul Society, was deeply aware of the misery and sufferings of the urban poor. For him the fundamental issue facing society was not political but social. Thus he wrote on one occasion:

> The problem that agitates the world today is not a matter of persons, nor a matter of political forms, but a social question; a war between those who have nothing and those who have too much.

In his understanding of the social problem and in his desire to do something about it, Ozanam once again differs from many of his fellow liberal Catholics. Most of them were members of the upper classes, hostile to the working-class movement because of the violence contained in it, defenders of liberty in the economic as well as the political areas of life.

As we have also seen, Ozanam's grasp of the existence of the problem did not extend to viable solutions. Charity, at least until the terrible events of 1848 opened his eyes to the depth of the problem, was his sole panacea. And yet the limitations of his answer to the issue of social justice did not include a pessimism as to the possibility of social amelioration.

This is the second element in his social Catholicism: a trust in social reform and in progress. The support for social reform by Christians is so much a part of the twentieth-century Church that we find it difficult to comprehend that this has not always been the case, although pessimism as to the possibility of material progress and reform has been the more traditional Christian view. For example, reform, as an effort to eliminate the root causes of poverty and other social evils, did not in general move medieval man; rather the emphasis was upon the necessity of enduring with Christian resignation the privations of the world. This is, of course, basically Christian in its understanding of the spiritual benefits of suffering, but until the liberal Catholic movement, it led to a passivity in the face of evils that are products of man and society, and that can in part be overcome.

The traditional view remained strong in the nineteenth-century Church, with many upper-class French Catholics, in the words of one historian, "the heirs of the temporal pessimism of Bossuet." Joseph DeMaistre, that most influential conservative thinker, took an extreme position on the connection between physical suffering and moral evil. For him, poverty, disease, and earthly misfortune were punishment for the sins of an individual, a family, or a nation. Needless to say, DeMaistre, a wealthy nobleman, did not have to endure poverty and other such social evils not because of his virtue but because of his good fortune in being born a member of the upper class. Louis Veuillot, although raised in poverty and a bitter foe of bourgeois society, still had little hope in the possibility of material improvement in society. Misery and privation seemed to him an inevitable part of our earthly existence, beyond any human efforts to alleviate. "Misery," he wrote, "is the law of God to which it is necessary to submit."

Ozanam never accepted this social pessimism, but held to the belief in progress and the consequent duty of Catholics to support social reform. In this he and those liberal Catholics who agreed with him were the precursors of a movement which has borne fruit in the twentieth-century Church. For when Ozanam places Catholicism on the side of social reform, he sounds a note that has been echoed grandly and sonorously by the French Church of our day.

When Ozanam writes of progress and improvement he clearly means not only that of the individual but also that of society as a whole. Conservatives, and indeed many other Christian thinkers throughout the centuries, would deny anything but individual improvement; taken as a whole, humanity cannot be shown to have progressed. This Ozanam emphatically disputes. "Humanity," he writes, "is made for progress." The admonition of the Gospel is "to be perfect as your heavenly Father is perfect." This, insists Ozanam, applies to social perfection as well as to the individual. Christianity not only teaches the possibility of social improvement, it makes it a moral precept. Catholics, then, must strive for social perfection, they must work for social reform and progress, just as conscientiously and wholeheartedly as they do for personal, moral improvement within themselves.

It is not that Ozanam, as an orthodox Christian, hoped to realize a perfect society in this world. The idea of social perfection was a goal toward which men should strive, not a consummation that would ever be attained. But the utopian nature of the goal did not mean that genuine progress toward it could not be made. Civilization, as far as Ozanam was concerned, had progressed. His interpretation of medieval history, discussed above, would be an example of social progress, for civilization, so he attempted to prove, had benefited and improved immeasurably through the influence of Christianity. On one occasion he wrote, "I see everywhere progress through Christianity." It was not only in the past that the evidence of progress was visible, but also in the present, and in the period prior to the revolution of 1848 there was a millenarian note in Ozanam's writing. A new age, in which society through the power and influence of Catholicism would reach to new heights, was, so he believed, about to commence. The world was on the verge of an epoch in which "would be realized the evangelical law in the social state, the epoch where the earthly city will be transfigured in order to become the city of God."

In this confidence in the mundane benefits of Christianity, in this optimism concerning the immediate worldly triumph of the Church, Ozanam fell into the error that lurks in liberal thought. If the conservative is often too pessimistic, too willing to forget the natural, social side of Christianity, the liberal, in his optimism, often places the material and the mundane above the spiritual and the supernatural. Ozanam, it is true, was aware of the danger of making Christianity simply a social reform movement, of naturalizing the message and the end of what is a supernatural religion. He warns, for instance, that we must be careful not to assume a "judaic point of view," which sees rewards and punishments, the Promised Land, as purely earthly concepts.

Furthermore, Ozanam is not interested in material progress for its own sake; it is moral improvement that attracted him, the victory of the spirit over the flesh. His disdain for purely material progress is illustrated by his reaction to the London Exhibition which he visited in 1851. This was the nineteenth-century equivalent of a twentieth-century American World's Fair, a presentation of the wonders of modern industry and technology. All of this marvelous evidence of the power of man over nature left Ozanam cold. In his letters from London he contrasts the abject poverty visible in that city with the opulence and marvels displayed at the Exhibition. The power over nature and the possibility of limitless prosperity demonstrated by the Exhibition brought to his mind the temptation of materialism and earthly power found in the New Testament: "Bow down and I will give all of this to you" was the phrase that came to his pen.

Granted that material progress for itself is not the end sought, nevertheless the development of industry and technology may be of advantage to the moral advance of mankind. Machines, for example, transform what had been handwork into the simple operation of watching and direction; they are examples of nature governed by thought and will. (Obviously Ozanam did not see the dehumanizing, impersonal character of machine work.) The advance of technology will, hoped Ozanam, create a situation where material needs will no longer occupy such an important place in the lives of men, a situation where men will have more leisure "in order to accomplish the glorious task of his moral perfection." Material progress, then, is of value as a means to an end, not as an end in itself.

Despite Ozanam's concern with moral rather than material progress, despite his awareness that our earthly society can never reach perfection, despite his warnings against making Christianity a social reform movement, still, at times, he tends to secularize the mission of Christianity, to overstate the material benefits and triumphs of his religion. This was especially true in the period before 1848, when under the influence of the successes of the Church and the liberal Catholic movement, his enthusiastic temperament led him to expect a great new age.

The events of the period prior to 1848 upon which Ozanam's hopes were fed were indeed remarkable from the point of view of the Church. In 1831, when Ozanam arrived in Paris, anticlericalism was rampant; seventeen years later, although the fundamental anticlericalism of French republicanism remained, a different popular attitude was apparent.

The evidence of this new attitude is widespread. When Archbishop de Quelen died an enormous crowd took part in his funeral procession; ten years earlier his residence had been sacked and he had been forced to go into hiding. In 1830 a priest in clerical garb in the streets of Paris was in danger of insult; ten years later Lacordaire appeared in the white robes of the Dominicans without incident. Nor was it simply a question of an end to hostility toward the Church, since there was also a revival of the practice of Catholicism among the French people. For instance, the Holy Week retreat and the Easter Communion at Notre Dame Cathedral, begun by the great Jesuit preacher, Père Ravignan, who had taken over the pulpit in the cathedral from Lacordaire, attracted thousands. Contemporary observers, including Ozanam, remark upon the number of prominent conversions as well as the large crowds which regularly attended religious services.

The new relationship between the Church and French society was reflected in the hierarchy. Archbishop de Quelen, a conservative and a royalist, came more and more to see the advantages of the liberal Catholic position. His successor, Archbishop Affre, supported Ozanam and his friends, and on occasions publicly endorsed Ozanam's words and actions. Père Lacordaire noticed with pleasure and surprise this radical change in the position of the hierarchy. As a former associate of Lamennais, he had personally felt the sting of the conservatism of the Church authorities. His description of the apparent liberalism of the French bishops was understandably ironic. He wrote to Ozanam of it in these words: "It is a case of crying with Joad: 'and what time was ever more fertile in miracles.'"

Ozanam, in his letters written after 1840, testifies also to the progress of Catholicism, not only in France but in the world at large. It was the election of Pope Pius IX in 1846 and the liberal policies of the new pope which most stimulated Ozanam's expectations of a great, new Christian age. He was in Rome when the new Pope took office. His letters from there describe in glowing terms the achievements of Pius IX and the magnificent future that awaits the Church under his leadership. "You will see," he wrote on one occasion to his brother, "that this will be the bishop of Rome who will once again reconcile the world to the papacy."

So it was that Ozanam reached a high pitch of enthusiasm and confidence in the future of Europe and the Church. It was not that he expected a miraculous immediate return of all the world to Catholicism, but that recent events had broken down the barrier and opened the way to a reconciliation of the Church and the world. The metaphor he used to describe his hopes was biblical. He compared the Church in modern society to the Jews crossing the desert on the march to the Promised Land. Just as the Chosen People had a leader given to them by God, Moses, so too the Church had Pius IX. Just as the Jews were forty years on the road to the Promised Land, so too the victory of the Church would follow only after years of toil and struggle. But just as the Israelites eventually reached their goal, so also the earthly triumph of the Church was assured.

The circumstances of the years immediately prior to 1848 were such that Ozanam's dream of a new Christian age did not seem fantastic; the reconciliation of the Church to the modern world upon which he had based his hopes was apparently within sight. It was at this moment that the cata-strophic events of 1848 intervened to end for almost a century the hope of reconciliation. How different might have been the history of the Church, of France, and of Europe had the open, positive attitude of Ozanam and his fellow liberal Catholics prevailed! Instead the story of the liberal Catholic movement of the nineteenth-century Church is a tragic tale of what might have been, a genuine tragedy in that at the very moment of apparent triumph the liberal Catholics saw their hopes crushed. It was not until a hundred years after 1848 that the French Church finally came to accept the liberal position. It is to the events of 1848, the results of which were the end of the expectations of Ozanam and his associates, that we must next turn.

Chapter VI   Pass to the Side of the Barbarians

The tragic developments of 1848 began with a civil war in Switzerland, but the spark that set Europe afire was lighted in the streets of Paris. Late in February, 1848, a street demonstration in the French capital became a revolution, and within three days, with little bloodshed and less regret, Louis-Philippe was on the road to an exile in England — in this case, a prosperous exile, since the prudent, thrifty, bourgeois monarch, having once experienced the inconstancy of the affections of the French people for the Bourbons, had invested his money abroad in preparation for just such an emergency. The flames of revolution soon spread throughout Europe; before the year was out the entire continent was ablaze. Kings were deposed, conservative statesmen forced into exile, and, eventually, the liberal, hitherto popular Pius IX, upon whom Ozanam had placed such high hopes, fled the Eternal City.

Regardless of the suddenness of the February uprising, the coming of revolution to France was no surprise. The July Monarchy had been punctuated at both ends by violent revolutions, with the people of Paris as the chief attendant at both its birth and its death. The eighteen years of its life were dotted by political and social unrest, for the July Monarchy saw much of what passes for politics in our modern world, abortive revolutions, extremist groups, terroristic activities, street demonstrations, and the like. Indeed, it was at this time that many of the techniques and methods of revolution and conspiracy were perfected.

Thus, for example, a new, popular profession was inaugurated at this time. One day the great bells of Notre Dame Cathedral began to ring, a traditional emergency signal to call the people into the streets. On this occasion, it was a group of conspirators who hoped to stimulate an uprising in the confusion caused by the unusual ringing of the bells. When the police reached the bell tower, only one of the conspirators remained. He was arrested and interrogated. When asked his profession, the arrested man replied, "I am a revolutionary," an answer that has sounded through the years as loud as the bells of Notre Dame on that day.

This first, self-styled revolutionary has had many heirs, some illustrious, some notorious, including Marx, Bakunin, Lenin, Trotsky, and Stalin. In the July Monarchy the most extraordinary, enthusiastic practitioner of the profession of revolution, if not its most successful, was Louis-Auguste Blanqui. Throughout his life, this mysterious "born conspirator," as he was described by the socialist, Louis Blanc, involved himself in secret, revolutionary activity. Since planned revolutions seldom succeed, Blanqui spent forty of his seventy-six years in prison. Ironically, this professional specialist in revolution was twice released from prison by spontaneous, unplanned uprisings. Despite his record of constant failure, Blanqui became the boogeyman of the French upper classes; for instance, the aristocratic Alexis de Tocqueville pictured Blanqui in 1848 as someone who "seemed to have passed his life in a sewer and to have just left it."

The extreme repugnance, even hatred felt for the July Monarchy by French republicans was often directed at the person of Louis-Philippe. This stout, elderly, clever, courageous, if colorless monarch deserves the dubious honor of being shot at more times than any French king in history. The spirit of the age, according to which recourse to violence was accepted as normal, is shown by the circumstances leading up to one of these attempted assassinations. The perpetrator of this particular crime, a retired army officer, disgusted with life, had decided to commit suicide. At the last moment, however, he changed his mind, with the intention of doing one last good act which would serve society, namely, to kill Louis-Philippe. In this isolated tragedy of good intentions applied to bad ends and worse means is written in large letters the story of many modern revolutionary movements.

The violence, the extreme methods and ideas of these French radicals have something psychological about them, although many of them were sincerely committed to justice for the lower classes. For example, Michel de Bourges, an intimate of the novelist George Sand, and a radical republican, shouted in the midst of one argument the following nihilistic sentiments:

> I tell you this corrupt society of yours will never be rejuvenated until this fine river runs red with blood, until that cursed palace is reduced to ashes, until the whole vast city at which we are looking has become a bare waste on which the poor man and his family can drive his plough and build his cottage.

When to the incendiary matter that was the misery and discontent of the working class is added the fiery spark of the nihilistic agitator, conflagration must soon follow. The July Monarchy sat upon this volatile pyre for eighteen years, and the surprise is not that it was eventually consumed but that it survived for so long.

This was the political and social world in which Ozanam lived, a world that was typically modern, if by this one understands what the twentieth century has exemplified: instability, violence, and revolution. The hope and confidence which Ozanam exuded then was not the product of a stable, healthy environment but rather the result of an inner peace and serenity. The trust in God that is at the basis of Ozanam's attitude toward his society was strong enough to overcome both the tensions in his world and an inward disposition to melancholy. It would be well if Christians of the troubled twentieth century would learn the secret of the peace of God in a world of violence from the example of Ozanam.

This serenity and strength which drew sustenance from a living faith was never better exemplified than in 1848. After the overthrow of Louis-Philippe, a provisional government was formed to rule France until a constitutional convention could be elected. This temporary arrangement continued throughout the spring of 1848, and for the two and a half months of rule by the provisional government, tension and the threat of a new revolution hung darkly over Paris. The members of the government itself were deeply divided over the issue of socialism, while the entire government was at the mercy of those who had made the February Revolution — the workers and students of Paris. Hence, March and April of 1848 were a period of fear, of disorder, with France trembling on the edge of another revolution.

Throughout these crisis-ridden weeks Ozanam maintained his optimism and his support of democracy. A few weeks before the February uprising he had presented, in an article that appeared in the Catholic newspaper, *Le Correspondent*, what was to be essentially his position during the difficult days that followed. The occasion for the article was the dis-

couragement and uneasiness of many Catholics over recent
developments outside of France, specifically over the uprising in Switzerland and disturbances in Italy. Some, fore-
casting the reaction of the majority of Catholics when
violence came to France, began to retreat to conservative
positions and to criticism of the liberal developments within
the Church. Although he did not usually write on contemporary political issues, Ozanam felt that he must answer these
critics in order to dispel this mist of discouragement; that
he was answering the call of duty is likely because there is
evidence that he wrote the article in response to a request
by Archbishop Affre.

The title of the essay, "The Danger and Hopes of Rome,"
indicates the theme. Ozanam made no effort to minimize
the perils facing Europe but, characteristically, he stressed
the positive, the hopes the future held if the liberal policies
of Pius IX prevailed. He presented in this article a thought
that runs through almost all of his writings dealing with the
modern world: namely, that contemporary society can be
compared to that of early medieval Europe. In each case an
old culture is dying, the death pangs of which are painful
and disturbing, but in dying, the old gives birth to the new.
Just as in the fifth century the fall of Rome meant the birth
of the culture of the Middle Ages, so in the nineteenth
century, the collapse of the old order will bring with it the
creation of a new one. Obviously, if the historical parallel
is in any way accurate, the youth of this new society was
likely to be troubled; hence, Ozanam realistically faced the
possibility of a period of instability and violence. The biblical
metaphor cited elsewhere will also serve here to illustrate
Ozanam's thought: it took the Israelites forty years to cross
the desert to the Promised Land; likewise the transition to
the new and better modern world will take time. What

Ozanam is telling his fellow Catholics "is to be patient as God is patient," but to look to the future with confidence for a happier time is in the offing.

Ozanam continued his historical comparison of the fifth and the nineteenth centuries by stressing the contribution of the Church to the formation of medieval culture. It was the popes and the saints of the Church who, in the centuries following the collapse of Rome, preserved civilization and made possible the flowering of the Christian High Middle Ages. Such is the duty of Catholics in the crisis of 1848; instead of discouragement, fear, and rejection of the new and radical elements, Catholics must look to these groups with sympathy and strive to bring out the Christian aspects of these innovations.

Specifically, what Ozanam has in mind is that Catholics must accept democracy, not simply as a political system, but as a new, popular, mass, egalitarian society. Once again to explain his thought, Ozanam refers to the fifth century. Just as the Church then put its trust in Clovis and the Franks, so in the nineteenth century it must place itself on the side of the people. Catholics, wrote Ozanam, in a phrase that horrified many, must "pass to the side of the barbarians."

He did not mean by this that Catholics should support the irresponsible extremists among the working class: "we will not be able perhaps," he admitted, "to convert Attila and Genseric." But what Ozanam did mean was that the Church and French Catholics must place their reliance and trust in the people, "pass to the side of the barbarians, that is to say from the camp of kings, of the statesmen of 1815, in order to go to the people."

If in the fifth century the Church had no choice if it were to survive, such was also the case in 1848. The reactionaries of 1848 are compared by Ozanam to the pagans of the fifth century, "who want to reign by force and the crushing of the spirit." This cannot, in the long run, succeed, because the future is in the hands of the people, in the hands of the barbarians, "and if there is nothing to hope for with these barbarians, we are at the end of the world."

Behind all of this is, at least by implication, Ozanam's providential view of history. St. Augustine saw the fall of Rome as a punishment upon decadent, immoral society, and Ozanam saw the crisis of 1848 as one of these great events by which God teaches and guides mankind. In this case, in Ozanam's liberal view, the direction in which God is moving humanity is upward, so that no matter how dark the night, he was confident that a brighter day would soon emerge. In his words, "I do not know if I am deceiving myself, but I believe that I can discern the beginnings of a divine plan which is unfolding."

This optimism in the face of political and social upheaval was not dimmed by the events of February and the weeks that followed. Throughout the dangerous days of the spring of 1848, when the existence of the government and of society itself hung by a thread as a new, more radical revolution threatened to erupt, Ozanam did not falter in his allegiance to the cause of the people. The street demonstrations of March, which very nearly turned into insurrection, made evident to him the immediate danger facing France. He wrote to his brother in April, for example, that "the last two months God had made it [life] so difficult that we have learned to hold on to only that which is necessary for our improvement and our salvation." This realization of the perilous situation in Paris did not, however, prevent him from continuing to stress the positive side of events and to defend the cause of the people.

There were encouraging signs to feed his optimism as the

twenty years of liberal Catholic activity were now bearing fruit. In 1830 the revolution had been against the king and the Church, in 1848 it was directed only at the monarchy. Ozanam noted this and took heart from it. He wrote to his brother in Lille that the churches had remained open during the fighting of February with no looting or damage done to them. He described how one of his friends, a priest, had been asked on numerous occasions to bless trees of liberty, planted as symbols of the victory of the Revolution.

Other contemporary observers remark on this sympathy between the Church and the Revolution. De Tocqueville observed that there was "a very general and unexpected return of a large part of the nation to religious things." At the same time, a Catholic newspaper reported that the street fighters of the February days went to Mass with the grime of battle still on their faces. Revolutionary pamphleteers and agitators spoke of Jesus, the proletariat of Nazareth, and announced that the victory of the Republic was the coming of the kingdom of God.

Likewise a new spirit existed within the Church, for the sympathetic, positive attitude of the hierarchy to modern trends was not killed by the February Revolution. Louis-Philippe's government had not been popular with the Church, while the moderation of the revolutionaries encouraged many churchmen to give at least tacit approval to the Revolution. Many bishops, indeed, officially recognized the new republican government, with Ozanam's patron, Archbishop Affre, leading the way. He permitted churches to be used as hospitals, held services for the dead after the fighting, and collected money for the wounded and for the widows of the slain. After the formation of the provisional government, Archbishop Affre promptly assured it of his support and that of his clergy.

Ozanam's writings, both public and private, in these crucial days when anarchy threatened, stress his confidence in the common people. Under the pressure of the crisis his sense of democracy grew, as the economic basis of the Revolution and of the discontent of the lower classes became clearer to him. He saw, with Marx and de Tocqueville, that the political ideal of the Revolution was peripheral, that the real Revolution was a social movement, with the issues of unemployment and wages the problems. In Ozanam's eyes, the French upper classes could not continue to ignore these vital matters of social justice.

His sympathy and attraction for the poor, unfortunate members of society led him to dwell upon their virtues. He contrasted the morality, the religion, the honesty of the poor, uneducated workers with the immoral, anti-Christian, materialistic propertied classes. The Church, he insisted, should shift its basis from the upper classes to the common people who are her natural allies. No French anticlerical republican ever wrote a more glowing panegyric of the people than Ozanam in the following words:

> The Church would do better to support herself upon the people, who are the true ally of the Church, poor as she, devout as she, blessed as she by all the benedictions of the Savior.

The frightful situation in which France and the Church found themselves in 1848 can be traced, according to Ozanam, to the failure of French Catholics to concern themselves with the common people. In one of his several letters to his priest brother, Alphonse, who was in Lille throughout these months, Ozanam suggested what the twentieth-century French Church eventually attempted: priests devoting themselves to the poor. Here is his advice to his brother and his fellow priests:

Busy yourselves always with the servants as well as with masters, and with workers as well as the rich; it is henceforth the only way of salvation for the Church in France. It is necessary that pastors give up their little bourgeois parishes, flocks of the elite in the midst of an immense population which they do not know.

Personally Ozanam devoted himself in those uncertain weeks to putting into practice his program of confidence in the people. He continued his charitable work with the poor, spoke often to clubs and groups in an effort to combat the radical social and economic ideologies that revolutionary Paris bred. He campaigned energetically for the election in April, 1848, of good men to the Constitutional Assembly. He supported Catholic candidates who had the courage and the conviction to defend democracy and the cause of the people. Eventually, under the urging of friends, he became a candidate himself to represent Lyon in the Assembly, his only venture into the political arena. Possibly because he did not decide until four days before the election, he was defeated, which, as he remarked, was probably for the best since neither his health nor his intellectual inclinations fitted him for the political world. At the same time, the efforts of Ozanam and his friends to elect deputies who shared their views were not entirely futile, for his close collaborator, Père Lacordaire, was chosen. Lacordaire, a striking figure in his white Dominican robes, sat on the far left of the Constitutional Assembly to indicate his support for democracy. He did not, however, influence the work of the Assembly, for he soon resigned his seat, foreseeing that this conservative, monarchial body would soon run head on against the discontent of the republican Parisian workers.

The most important contribution that Ozanam made to the cause of Christian democracy in 1848 was his participation in the publication of a new Catholic periodical. In

March, 1848, he and several other leading Catholic liberals, including Lacordaire and the Abbé Maret, disturbed by the failure of Catholics to support democracy, decided to publish a newspaper that would serve as an answer to the conservative columns of *L'Univers*. The newspaper, a weekly for most of its existence, first appeared in mid-April, 1848, and continued until the middle of the following year, although Lacordaire resigned from it late in the summer of 1848 and Ozanam contributed little after the end of 1848.

The title chosen for the new periodical is significant, *L'Ere Nouvelle* (*The New Era*), and its program and policies can be gathered from an editorial that appeared in its first issue:

> The nation wants the Republic. Why should we prevent it? Is it that the Gospel or the Church ever forbade such a form of government? What divine reason is there to oppose the establishment of a republic in France? Assuredly none. . . .

> We can expect that the Republic will employ its power in the relief of the miseries of the greatest number of its children. . . . We expect also from it that it will take under its protection the people who lost their nationality by unjust conquests.

It was, in brief, a Catholic journal devoted to democracy and social reform; in the language of the day, it was a spokesman for the party of confidence, confidence in the people and in the future. As the fear and hostility of the majority of French Catholics toward the cause of democracy and reform increased, *L'Ere Nouvelle* and its editors became the targets of more and more bitter attacks. Despite this animosity, Ozanam wrote in it often during the summer and fall of 1848 and continued to support it until it ceased publication.

How much influence *L'Ere Nouvelle* had on the course of events is questionable, although in May and June of 1848 it had the largest circulation of any Catholic newspaper in Paris. Furthermore, the vehemence of the attacks of its enemies would indicate that it posed some threat to the conservative position. Its greatest significance does not depend upon its success or failure but lies simply in the fact that a Catholic newspaper, with prominent intellectual and religious figures participating, stood boldly and confidently on the side of the people through all the vicissitudes of 1848. The importance of this becomes greater when placed in juxtaposition to the increasingly conservative and authoritarian position of most French Catholics.

The uneasy truce that prevailed in France through March and April ended in May 1848. The event that signaled a new outburst of violence was the convening of the Constitutional Assembly which had been elected in April. The elections had turned out surprisingly conservative, with the majority of delegates opposed to republicanism and social reform. France had repudiated Paris! Clearly French Catholics had not heeded Ozanam's pleas; they had not passed to the side of the people but had remained in the camp of kings. Alexis de Tocqueville, frightened by the specter of social democracy, describes for us with evident approval how the people in his district of provincial France marched off to vote behind the parish priest. Order, authority, and property were surely the catchwords that attracted French Catholics in 1848, not liberty, equality, and fraternity, as Ozanam would have had it.

That the Parisian workers would react strongly to this conservative triumph was certain, for, if anything, the excitement and discontent among them had increased since the February Revolution. Paris, in the weeks following the overthrow of Louis-Philippe, had a plethora of radical pamphleteers and agitators broadcasting their extravagant theories. Furthermore, the workers of Paris, conscious that it was they who had overthrown the July Monarchy, with their hopes raised by this triumph, would hardly stand by quietly and peacefully amid the utter destruction of their expectations. Finally, the economic situation was more difficult than ever, for the disorders of the Revolution had injured trade and industry. Unemployment increased steadily, to such an extent that the provisional government had recourse to National Workshops, a kind of works relief program from which the unemployed received at least some income.

The first act in the tragic denouement of the French Revolution of 1848 was played on May 15, when a mob invaded the meeting place of the newly elected Constitutional Convention. For a short time this unruly antagonistic crowd dominated the Convention, but the National Guard, which remained loyal to the government, eventually cleared the building at bayonet point. The results of this chaotic fiasco were that most of the radical leaders of the workers were arrested, including Blanqui, while the delegates to the Convention as well as those who supported them, disgusted and terrified by the actions of the Parisian lower classes, became more conservative.

This increased hostility to the workers on the part of the Convention was made clear in the second act of the drama when the government decided to close the National Workshops. There were good reasons to eliminate eventually this form of relief; aside from the traditional bourgeois arguments concerning the drain on the public treasury and the idleness of the workers as a result of public assistance, the National Workshops were attracting many questionable persons from the provinces so that they were becoming centers of agitation. But to do so in the tension-ridden circumstances of the summer of 1848 was either ineptitude or a deliberately provocative action. Be that as it may, this was precisely what the government did, turning thousands of unemployed workers into the streets with no prospects, in the unsettled conditions of the day, of finding work.

For a couple of weeks after the closing of the Workshops, the working-class districts of Paris smoldered sullenly in the June sun, waiting for the final act of the tragedy to be played. Few doubted that a conflict must ensue, but for a brief time there was an intermission, a pause before the final, conclusive battle began.

Late in June barricades appeared in the poorer sections of the city as the workers prepared for battle. The government responded by declaring martial law, placing General Cavaignac, a tough, able soldier who had fought in Algeria, in command. Then, with the inevitability of a Greek drama, the fighting commenced. No individual, no group, no particular locale can be cited as the focal point of the first fighting. It was as if both sides were carrying out predetermined rules, as though the battle began without any conscious intentions or actions by the participants.

For four days the conflict raged. It was not so much an attempt by the workers to seize control of Paris, as a siege of the working-class districts by the army. Block by block, barricade by barricade, in the warm June weather, broken by an occasional heavy thunderstorm, the soldiers gradually reduced the workers' fortress. Men, women, and children fought silently, grimly, without leaders, against the attacks of the troops. Alexis de Tocqueville, an observer of these events, described in gripping words the character of the fighting:

> I come at last to the insurrection of June, the most extensive and the most singular that has occurred in our history, and perhaps in any other: the most extensive because during four days, more than a hundred thousand men were engaged in it;

the most singular, because the insurgents fought without a war-cry, without leaders, without flags, and yet with a marvellous harmony and an amount of military experience that astonished the eldest officer.

De Tocqueville might also have added that the June Days were unique in that this was class war in its purest form, to a degree unknown in any such previous event. It was the workers of Paris against the rest of France. Both de Tocqueville and Ozanam had called attention to the social nature of the events leading up to the February Revolution, that the issue was poor against rich, workers against bourgeois. The developments from February to June had greatly deepened this class division. The class nature of the June insurrection was exemplified when a middle-class intellectual, known to be sympathetic to the workers, approached one of the barricades in an effort to end the fighting. He was received politely, but one of the defenders said to him: "You do not know what misery is, you have never been hungry."

Once France united behind the government, the defeat of the workers was assured, and, after bitter fighting, the army gained control of the city. Not unexpectedly, the punishment meted out to the defeated was severe, with executions, exile, and imprisonment the fate of a large number of the June revolutionaries. Much more serious was the effect of the June Days upon the minds of Frenchmen. On the one hand, the class consciousness of the Paris working class became much stronger, a legacy upon which twentieth-century French Communism still feeds; on the other, the rest of French society, peasant, bourgeois, aristocrat, became increasingly conservative.

Chapter VII   A Charitable Agitation

The events of June, 1848, were particularly trying for Ozanam. The public tragedy was compounded for him by a personal loss when his father-in-law, to whom he was very close, died at this time. Furthermore, his understanding and defense of the cause of the workers made his sorrow over the uprising doubly great. Still his sympathy for the poor and his insight into the justice of their demands did not lead him to espouse so radical a solution as the June insurrection. He was too moderate a man, too attached to law and order to defend an anarchic, violent movement such as this. For him there could be no question that the defeat of the workers was a necessity for France and for civilization. At the same time, the bloodshed of those days, the armed resistance of the working class to legal authority, seemed to have ended his hopes for a peaceful transition to Christian democracy.

If he did not give way to despair in the midst of his personal sorrow and the collapse of his hopes for his society, it was because of his trust in Providence. His mood is shown by a letter he wrote immediately subsequent to the June Days in which he said in part: "We are a poor family under the judgment of God! In the cloud of sorrow in which we live, I no longer see where Providence leads us. . . ." But Ozanam's optimism, his hope for the future, was not entirely extinguished by the flood of violence. He again asserted, in the midst of the chaos of the summer of 1848, his confidence in Christian democracy, but now he expected the road to the attainment of such a society to be long and rocky. He wrote of this:

> I have always believed in the invasion of the barbarians; I believe it now more than ever. I believe it will be long and murderous, but destined sooner or later to be brought under the Christian law, and by consequence to regenerate the world. Only, I am sure that we will witness all the horror of the battle. I do not know if our children will live long enough to see the end of it.

Ozanam's commitment to the cause of Christian democracy did not prevent him from taking an active role in opposing the June rebellion. He was a member of the Parisian National Guard, a militia formed in April, 1848, consisting principally of men from the upper classes and, as a member, was under arms during the fighting of June. No one was less fitted physically and temperamentally for the work of a soldier, but, feeling it to be a duty, Ozanam served willingly. Happily, as he himself admits, he did not have to take an active part in the conflict but remained on guard duty away from the scene of action throughout the fighting.

One can imagine the painful thoughts that must have passed through his mind as the intensity and ferocity of the battle increased. The pall of smoke hanging over the city, the sounds of musket and cannon fire, the cries of the combatants, and the silent, deserted street corner at which he stood guard must all have eaten deeply into his sensitive and sympathetic nature. It was in this mood of helplessness and despair, with Ozanam and several friends who were with him in the National Guard desperately searching their minds for some way of ending the fighting, that it was decided that they would ask Archbishop Affre to intervene.

Nothing indicates better the reconciliation of the Church and the working class than this decision of Ozanam and his friends. Obviously, for the mediation of the archbishop to have any hope of success, it was first necessary that the rebels have veneration and respect for the Church and for the hierarchy. Eighteen years before, at the time of the revolution of 1830, the unpopularity of the Church was such that many bishops went into hiding. It is to his credit as well as to the success of the efforts of the liberal Catholics that Archbishop Affre dared to attempt mediation.

Once Ozanam and his friends had made their decision they proceeded to the archbishop's residence to present their suggestion to him. They found the archbishop receptive; indeed, he told them that he had been contemplating such an action himself. This must have been a very difficult decision for Affre. Although he had publicly supported many liberal Catholic policies and had worked to reconcile the Church with the lower classes, still he was a reserved, retiring, perhaps even timid personality, with a horror of violence and conflict. His state of mind after agreeing to attempt arbitration was such that he went to confession as one about to die.

Upon the insistence of Ozanam and others, the archbishop put on his full robes of office, further evidence of their assurance that he would be received with respect by these desperate, violent men. Accompanied by Ozanam and his fellow guardsmen, the archbishop passed through the streets of Paris to the cheers and applause of all who saw him. He received permission from General Cavaignac to attempt mediation, although the general warned him of the danger of his mission, pointing out that a military officer who had tried the same thing had been killed. Affre, however, would not be deterred from what he considered to be his duty, but proceeded to the scene of the fighting. When he arrived at the barricade at the Palace de la Bastille, the center of the conflict, he asked the commander of the troops there to stop firing, saying, "I will go alone to these unhappy people." Affre then ordered Ozanam and the others to remain behind, although they had asked to accompany him on his peace mission, and moved forward toward the barricade. Led by a young man waving a white flag, Affre reached the barricade where he was quickly surrounded by a great number of soldiers and insurgents. He mounted the barricade and was in the act of speaking words of reconciliation to the crowd when a roll of drums was heard. This was taken by both sides as a signal to resume firing, and, in the confusion, a bullet struck the archbishop in the chest. The rebels carried the mortally wounded man into a nearby house with evident signs of grief and sorrow. A doctor was summoned, but the archbishop died a few days later, his last words being, "Let my blood be the last shed."

Thus died Archbishop Affre, a martyr to the cause of reconciliation among all Frenchmen. Although his effort at mediation was a tragic failure, nevertheless it is agreed by all that the death of the prelate was an accident and that he was mourned by the insurgents as well as by the rest of France. Twenty-three years later, in another uprising by the radical elements in Paris, the so-called Paris Commune, a successor of Archbishop Affre to the see of Paris was seized by the revolutionaries as a hostage. When the revolution collapsed, the archbishop and many of his clergy were murdered in cold blood by the rebels. The violent death of these two holders of the episcopal see of Paris in the course of the nineteenth century led one historian to suggest that it must have been the most dangerous post in the Catholic Church. (In 1857 a third archbishop of Paris was killed by an assassin.) Aside from this, the significance in these two tragedies lies in their differences. Both men died martyrs, but the first died accidentally, mourned in death by all Frenchmen, and during his life so widely respected that he could seek to mediate a bloody civil war. The second of these martyred archbishops, just as sincerely devoted to his people as his predecessor, was murdered by members of his diocese out of hatred for the Church. Surely nothing is stronger evidence of the collapse of the influence and popularity of the Church among the Parisian working class than the contrast in these two events.

In the weeks following the June Days, Paris resembled a city under siege; patrols roamed the streets, troops camped in the parks, and martial law prevailed. In that summer the trials of the June insurgents dominated the scene, with the punishments delivered against them often quite severe. Although the radical movement was seriously injured, the fear of a new uprising was in the minds of most Frenchmen. Indeed, occasional street riots and demonstrations did occur, but they were weak, abortive affairs. For the most part they deserve little attention; one of them, however, produced an incident that merits telling. In 1849 a sudden, spontaneous street riot took place. As the crowd moved wildly through the streets, one of its supposed leaders, Ledru-Rollin, caught by surprise, was seated in a cafe. Seeing the crowd, he leaped to his feet, exclaiming, "I must follow them, I am their leader," a cry that goes far to explain the leadership in many modern, popular movements.

The appearance of a besieged city that was Paris in the summer of 1848 was reflected in the minds of many Frenchmen. The fear of a new revolution and the horror of the remembrance of the past led France to become more and more conservative. The results of the presidential election of December, 1848, show this conclusively. At this time the nation voted to choose a president for the newly created Second Republic. The candidates included the radical leader, Ledru-Rollin, the victor of June Days, General Cavaignac, and Louis Napoleon, the nephew of Napoleon Bonaparte. The latter won an overwhelming victory although he was practically unknown in France, having lived most of his life outside its boundaries. But Louis Napoleon, as the heir of Napoleon I, was in the minds of most Frenchmen the symbol of authority, order, and a strong man in control. This was what France eagerly sought after the chaos of 1848, even at the cost of liberty and democracy. And this was precisely the price that they were asked to pay, for within four years Louis Napoleon had himself declared emperor, and as Napoleon III ruled France until 1870.

Foremost among Frenchmen in this move to conservatism were the Catholics. The hostility to republicanism, to popular movements, to the ideals of the French Revolution that had prevailed among them prior to 1830 was back in full vigor. Liberty, social reform, and democracy, always suspect in the minds of nineteenth-century French Catholics, now came to mean revolution, socialism, and anarchism. Once again many Catholics believed that religion required a strong government, the defense of property and of the status quo.

The conservatism prevalent among French Catholics after 1848 was greatly intensified by the events which took place in Rome. As we have seen, Pius IX, after his election in 1846, adopted a liberal policy in the government of the

Papal States, much to the joy of Ozanam. But the revolutionary, nationalistic spirit of the day placed the Pope in an impossible dilemma. It was impossible for him to satisfy the demand of radical groups for a republican government for Rome and the Papal States, nor could he cooperate in a war to unite Italy, since the chief enemy would be Catholic Austria. Consequently, with the outbreak of the revolution of 1848 in Italy, Pius IX's popularity with the radicals and liberals in Italy came to a sudden end. Disorder and strife became widespread in the Papal States and particularly in Rome itself. The lay prime minister of the Papal States, who had been appointed by the Pope in an effort to satisfy the demand for a liberal government, was stabbed to death in the streets of Rome. Later a bishop was killed by a bullet while standing next to the Pope. Finally, unable to keep order, Pius IX fled Rome, leaving the republican followers of Mazzini in control.

The reaction of French Catholics, including those with liberal leanings, was quite strong. Few nineteenth-century Catholics could conceive of the Pope without the Papal States, for it was felt that the independence of the head of the universal Church required that he govern Rome. Furthermore, the methods used against Pius IX — assassination, violence, and revolution — were considered an affront to all Catholics.

Eventually, in 1849, the Pope was restored to the control of Rome by a French army. Louis Napoleon, in response to the demands of French Catholics, and in the hope of insuring their support for his government, decided to oppose Italian republicanism and to support the Pope. After a relatively difficult battle, French troops overcame the Roman republic and returned Pius to his domain. French soldiers remained in the Eternal City, and the alliance between authoritarian government and the French Church was cemented. In passing it might be noted that Pope Pius IX personally shed his liberalism after the revolution of 1848 to become extremely conservative, a further cause of the movement of French Catholics to the Right.

In France, in the post-1848 reaction, fear of radicalism bordered on the hysterical. General Cavaignac, hardly a radical, remarked that to give money to a beggar was enough to bring on the suspicion of socialism. *Le Correspondent*, a Catholic magazine that had supported the liberal movement before 1848, wrote in 1849 that the cause of religion and property were inextricably connected. Even Armand de Melun, the apostle of the poor, showed his disgust with the lower classes when he wrote that all the efforts to help them had not prevented the poor from involving France in a terrible carnage.

The extreme antipathy of most French Catholics to working-class demands and to social reform in the post-1848 period is best exemplified by Montalembert. As a prominent liberal Catholic, Montalembert was, prior to 1848, in sympathy with at least some of the reform movement. It is true that his liberalism never extended to democracy, to support for popular agitation, and the events of 1848 strengthened his mistrust of the lower classes. Indeed, after this exciting year, because of his fear of new uprisings, Montalembert accepted and defended restrictions upon liberty which would have horrified him earlier. He justified this switch by the assertion that post-1848 France was sick to death from a false liberty. His pessimism concerning the future of France contrasted strongly with the optimism of Ozanam and his friends. The following quotation from Montalembert shows his state of mind after the revolution:

I need not, even if I had the time, enter into details about the state of France and of Europe; we are all progressing onwards to the bottomless pit of socialism which is nothing else but the logical conclusion of Protestantism and democracy. Nothing, I am convinced, can or will save us. Thanks to Louis Bonaparte, we shall have a short halt on the road, but we shall ere long move on. As you most justly say, the day of Europe is past; she has sinned too deeply to be forgiven. Every power but the Church will be utterly destroyed. . . .

It is in the light of this Catholic conservatism, this antipathy to the demands for social reform, this willingness to give up liberty for order, that Ozanam's reaction to the events of 1848 must be seen. As might be expected, the tragic events of that year, especially the bloodshed of June, had a profound effect upon his mind. But Ozanam was never led by the violence of the lower classes to forget the justice of their cause. His horror at the June Days did not lead him to surrender his belief in the future of Christian democracy. He continued, as he wrote to a more conservative friend, Foisset, in September, 1848, "to believe in the possibility of Christian democracy." The chaos and uncertainty of the first half of 1848 did not bring him to desert the party of confidence in the future and in the people. If Montalembert, as in the quotation cited, to justify his pessimism can appeal to Providence to punish a sinful Europe, it is Ozanam's trust in God which permits him to view the future with hope. It is true that the disasters of 1848 taught him that the progress and the triumph of the good in his society, which he so eagerly anticipated, were not to be immediately realized. Still his unshakable belief that Providence watches over mankind, that the events of history are God's plan for man, gave Ozanam a serenity and a confidence that most of his contemporaries lacked. Thus, in words that answer Montalembert's forebodings, he counseled Frenchmen against giving in to despair and "by announcing the ruin of the country, to help cause it." In brief, Ozanam avoided the traps that ensnared most French Catholics in 1848. He did not forget the fundamental justice of the demands of the workers, despite his repugnance for the extreme methods adopted to attain these demands. At the same time, he refused to give up in despair over the future prospects of his society.

It was not that Ozanam sympathized with the social program advanced by the leaders of the radical element in French society. He shared with most upper-class Frenchmen a horror and fear of popular revolution, doubtless a heritage of the Jacobin Terror of 1794, which lingered in their minds like the remembrance of a childhood nightmare. He wrote, for example, in *L'Ere Nouvelle* of September, 1848, congratulations to the "honest people" of France who had crushed the uprising and saved the nation. The primary responsibility for the catastrophe of June rested, in Ozanam's view, with the irresponsible, radical leaders of the workers. Likewise, he did not scruple to write after the June Days that much of the misery of the poor resulted from their ignorance and from the immoralities of their lives. He also made clear in an article written in August for *L'Ere Nouvelle* that he opposed socialism. This doctrine as preached in 1848 was, for Ozanam, both antisocial and anti-Catholic in that it struck at the two institutions necessary for society: the family and property. Clearly, then, his continued support for social reform and for democracy did not stem from an agreement with the extreme, radical social philosophy of the workers, but from an understanding of the need for justice as well as an awareness that the future was in the hands of the people.

Nor did the events outside France satisfy Ozanam's expectations any better. No Catholic had placed greater hopes in Pius IX than Ozanam; no Catholic had supported the liberal policies of the Pope to a greater degree than he. The Roman revolution of 1848 put an end to all this, to the dreams of a soon-to-come glorious era for France and for the Church. Still, Ozanam did not revert to conservatism, did not give up his liberalism, did not become pessimistic, although his understanding of the present and future of his society became more profound and more Christian.

Ozanam's personal knowledge of the lives of the Parisian poor, gained from his work as a Vincentian, along with his sympathy for them had led him to the realization that the crises of 1848 were fundamentally economic in origin. If the workers had erred in following wicked, radical leaders, the causes of their discontent were real and grievous. In a series of articles written first for Le Correspondent and later, after June, for L'Ere Nouvelle, Ozanam attempted to convince his fellow French Catholics of the reality of the misery of the life of the lower classes. That he was preaching to deaf ears, to men who would not listen to the truth, does not detract from the nobility of his effort.

His goal in these articles was clear: in his words, "to begin and to maintain among Christians, a *charitable agitation* against the evil that has troubled a free people for fifty years, and which will henceforth be its shame." Shortly after the February revolution Ozanam began his "charitable agitation" in an article in Le Correspondent in which he argued that the working class had been betrayed by the middle class after the revolution of 1830. In the eighteen years since that event, the French upper classes refused to consider the basic problem of employment for the workers. Now, insisted Ozanam, it is the duty of Catholics to study this question, to seek for the lower classes satisfactory working conditions, a full life, and a peaceful old age.

After the June Days Ozanam continued his journalistic campaign for social justice for the workers. His presentation of their case was especially strong in an article entitled "To Honest People," which appeared in *L'Ere Nouvelle* in September, 1848. After congratulating France on its victory over the June insurgents, Ozanam warned that a victory achieved by force was not enough; it was imperative also that the causes of the uprising be eliminated. The defeat of the rebels would prove a transitory victory without the conquest of a more dangerous enemy, "an enemy that you do not know enough about, of whom you do not like to talk, and of whom we are determined to speak to you today: MISERY."

A large part of the remainder of the article consists of a presentation of the stark misery which existed in the poorer sections of Paris in the weeks following the June Days. He cites statistics: that two months after the end of the fighting, there are two hundred and sixty-seven thousand people in the city who are suffering from hunger; that in one of the districts where the uprising had occurred, seventy thousand of the ninety thousand inhabitants require public assistance in order to survive.

More moving, if less precise, is his description of the situation of these unhappy people painted from his personal visits to the homes of the poor. As always with Ozanam, it was not enough to write and to observe, one must also act. Consequently, in the weeks following the June Days, he devoted himself to charitable works. Very likely he was a member of the group organized by de Melun to assist the vanquished workers and their families. This committee, which included members of the St. Vincent de Paul Society, divided the poverty-stricken area of Paris into districts with a group of men responsible for each. Although Ozanam does not tell us that he was active in the work of this committee, it can be surmised that his connection with the St. Vincent de Paul Society as well as his constant involvement in charitable endeavors would have led him into this group. He was assuredly busy aiding the poor at this time; whether with this committee or through some other organization is of little matter.

Thus it was that the description of the life of the poor in the articles in *L'Ere Nouvelle* was based upon personal observation and experience. This fact, combined with his deep sympathy for the poor as well as his literary talent, make them a powerful and moving plea for these unfortunate people. It was from the article, "To Honest People," that the picture of the Parisian poor quoted in an earlier chapter was taken. As this excerpt shows, Ozanam pictured in graphic, gripping words the miserable dwellings of the workers, the lack of food and fresh air, the debilitating effect of disease, and the early deaths of many of the children of the poor. His failure to move his fellow Catholics to action was not the result of an inability to make known to them the plight of the urban poor.

Ozanam, in these various articles, attempted also to suggest remedies for the grievous ulcer that was troubling French society. Unfortunately he was much better at diagnosing the illness than at prescribing a cure. This is so, in part, because he considered the illness — poverty — to be so ingrained in society that it could never be entirely removed. Also, as a pious, spiritual man, Ozanam was quite conscious of the benefits that can accrue from poverty, both to those who suffer it in a spirit of resignation and to those who attempt to alleviate it by charity. It is also true that Ozanam, despite the contemporary charges of radicalism made against him, was a middle-class Catholic, a moderate, balanced personality whose social philosophy reflected this background. He was opposed to socialism, and there is very little indication in his writings that he looked to the government to play any large role in overcoming the problem of poverty. Essentially, even after 1848, he relied upon charity; in these articles, for instance, he called for "a crusade of charity," to be led by the French clergy. He stressed that the rich had an obligation to use their surplus wealth to aid the poor, and he called for a national subscription as an immediate answer to the problems created by the chaos and disorders of 1848. Surely these are but patchwork, feeble remedies when offered as a cure to the massive illness of poverty and misery that faced French society, but one will look in vain to Ozanam for a profound or viable answer to the social problem.

It can be said for him that he was not alone in his failure to provide satisfactory answers in this area for better economists and social philosophers than Ozanam proved unequal to the task. Furthermore, in these journalistic writings, produced under the stress of crisis, one can glean some occasional remarks that make it appear that Ozanam was groping toward a more meaningful, satisfactory solution than charity. For example, in the article written for *Le Correspondent* before the June Days, his words can be interpreted as a call for social justice and for the reform of socioeconomic institutions. He makes clear here that it is a question of justice, not simply of charity; that Catholics must remember their obligations to man as well as to God. In other words, Ozanam demands that Christians fulfill their social duties as well as their spiritual. There are also some indications that Ozanam was becoming increasingly aware that some basic reform of the political and economic institutions of society would be necessary before the problem of poverty could be solved. He wrote in the article in Le *Correspondent* that Catholics must strive to improve society "not only by the charity required of man, but by our efforts to obtain the institutions that will free them [the workers] and make them better."

These, then, were his suggestions as to how to deal with the socioeconomic problem which lay at the root of the disorder of 1848. And, indeed, after the June Days, even this meager program is no longer mentioned as Ozanam returns once more to charity and the political goal of democracy as the methods to be used to avoid a repetition of the violence of 1848. Still, granted the limitations in his social philosophy, most of which were inherent in his society and his background, his campaign of "charitable agitation" to awaken the consciences of French Catholics to the misery of their fellow countrymen was a noble if futile endeavor.

Chapter VIII   The Will of Providence

The last years of Ozanam's life, the five years from 1848 until his death in 1853, were a period of sorrow and lost hopes. The post-1848 conservative reaction meant the end of his expectations for an early victory for liberalism. Because Ozanam refused to give up his faith in liberalism, it also meant that he lived the last years of his life suspect in the eyes of many French Catholics, the victim of bitter personal attacks on his character and his orthodoxy. Finally, he suffered from constant ill health throughout these years, a double trial for him since it prevented him completing his scholarly work at which he had so long labored. His response to this time of troubles is the theme of this chapter.

To appreciate fully the utter collapse of his hopes for an early victory of his political ideals, the situation prior to 1848 must be recalled. As we have seen, the liberal Catholic movement was riding the crest in the 1840's. The reconciliation with the modern world for which it stood was becoming increasingly acceptable to the hierarchy, culminating in the election of Pius IX. The political connotations of this religious liberalism were also gaining a hold with Catholics, as

liberty, constitutional government, and the reform of institutions were no longer considered dangerous. Democracy, it
is true, was still a radical, suspect doctrine, although Christian democrats, such as Ozanam, remained respected and
influential. Catholics, like most Frenchmen, were hostile to
any extreme social theories, either being content with traditional solutions to the problem of poverty or uninterested
in the lot of the poor. Even here, however, the pre-1848
situation, insofar as it affected the Church, was improving,
because the liberalism of Catholics as well as the extensive
charitable work of members of the Church brought a novel
popularity to Catholicism among the working class.

All of this worked to fire the ardent, enthusiastic temperament of Ozanam to a high pitch of optimism. His trust in
and understanding of the work of Providence in human
affairs, which at this time stressed too strongly the immediate, mundane benefits of divine intervention in the affairs
of man, led him to expect, if not the millennium, at least
a great new Christian age.

That Ozanam's hopes were, if not ill-founded, premature
by nearly a century was suddenly brought home by the revolutions of 1848. Clearly the newly planted tree of liberalism
had as yet no deep roots in the soil of the French Church
so that it was unable to withstand the tempest of 1848.
Consequently the events of 1848 abruptly altered the status
of Ozanam's dream of reconciling the Church to modern
society. No longer was his liberalism riding the tide, no
longer was the direction in which the French Church was
moving congenial to Ozanam's views; henceforth he was
forced to swim against the current.

Social and religious developments after 1848 did little to
aid him in his battle against the predominating conservative
current. In France the authoritarianism of Louis Napoleon

became more firmly entrenched as French Catholics continued their support of him. Within the Church itself, a strong antiliberal movement grew, headed by the erstwhile liberal, Pius IX, so that, in general, the Church returned to its defensive posture in regard to the world, to its suspicion of liberalism, democracy, and reform.

None of this led Ozanam to change his views. He remained convinced that democracy was the political ideal of the future. Despite the violence of 1848, he continued to insist that Catholics, if they were to perform their mission in the world, must "pass to the side of the barbarians." Nor did he see any reason to alter his position that Christianity had to be presented in a positive, attractive manner if it were to appeal to the numerous unbelieving and doubting elements of modern society. Nevertheless, the failure of the liberal movement, the growing conservatism of Catholics, and the estrangement of the Church from the world made Ozanam's last years difficult, particularly because of the personal attacks that were made upon him because of his continued adherence to liberalism.

Since Ozanam did not trim his sails to fit the times, he became an object of suspicion to many of his fellow Catholics. His old foes of *L'Univers* returned to the attack with new vigor. Aided by the antiliberal current of post-1848 France, which gave Veuillot and his associates sharper arrows for their quivers, the newspaper now impugned not only his political and social ideas but his religious orthodoxy as well. Although this was only to be expected, the unhealthy miasma of suspicion and rumor spread far beyond the adherents of *L'Univers* until it reached old friends and associates.

The bitterest of these personal attacks launched by *L'Univers* came in 1850, when the specter of bad health was already throwing its dark shadow over Ozanam's life. Two incidents brought on this onslaught. The first of these was an obituary that Ozanam had written for his old friend and patron, Ballanche. In the course of the article, he praised both Ballanche and Chateaubriand for their contributions to the Catholic cause. It was this that first called down the wrath of *L'Univers*.

Although both of these men had died piously within the Church, there were incidents in their lives that were open to criticism from a Catholic point of view. Chateaubriand had not always lived an exemplary life and had expressed sentiments that were of questionable orthodoxy. Ballanche, on the other hand, was a good, sincere Catholic throughout his life, but had on occasions advanced unorthodox views; for example, he had at one time denied the existence of hell. Ballanche later recanted this, and both he and Chateaubriand, as Ozanam pointed out at the time, had made great contributions in the course of their lives to the cause of religion. Nevertheless, *L'Univers* used Ozanam's eulogy of these two men as one of the bases of their attack upon him.

To this was added a difference over the Inquisition. The Catholic conservative newspaper had defended and praised this institution in its columns. Obviously the defense of this harsh, medieval ecclesiastical court would serve only to turn nineteenth-century Frenchmen away from the Church. Likewise, it was further ammunition for the French anticlerical charge that Catholicism and tyranny must necessarily go together. It was for these reasons that Ozanam opposed *L'Univers*. As he wrote privately of the newspaper, "I detest its opinions; I know the evil they do." His aim was to make clear that all Catholics did "not belong to this violent school of which *L'Univers* has become the spokesman." But Ozanam did not make it a personal matter; he did not, for instance, mention either the newspaper or its editors by name in his public writings.

L'Univers was not so careful in its response to Ozanam. In an unsigned article, the newspaper accused him of holding heretical views and of deserting the Catholic cause. As was *pro forma* with *L'Univers*, it also took the opportunity to suggest that Ozanam's motives in deserting the Church were ignoble and selfish, namely, the hope of advancing his academic career at the secular University of Paris.

Naturally such baseless and venemous accusations were a severe trial to one as sensitive as Ozanam. But the really painful blow came when an old friend from Lyon, Dufieux by name, after reading the article in *L'Univers*, wrote to express his shock at Ozanam's denial of his religious faith. Dufieux, to judge from this incident, must have been one of those honest, unimaginative busybodies who do not realize the harm that they do. To write directly and without warning to a very old, close friend to inquire if he had given up his religion for the most ignoble and cynical of motives when the only evidence for this is an article in an extremely partisan, unreliable newspaper requires a degree of fatuity almost beyond comprehension.

This unexpected, shocking letter from his old friend brought a cry of anguish from Ozanam. "Here I am," he wrote, "at thirty-seven worn out in the service of my faith." What made the blow so painful was that one who knew him so well would give any credence to the charge. "You who know me so well," lamented Ozanam, "to whom I opened the innermost recesses of my heart . . . [yet] a denunciation in a newspaper is enough to make you doubt my faith."

He then goes on to explain to his doubting friend, unnecessarily it would seem, that to praise Ballanche and Chateaubriand, to recognize their great contributions to Catholicism, does not mean that one subscribes to all of their sentiments and opinions. He insists, even more unnecessarily, one would think, in a letter to an old friend, that any academic success he may have had did not come from "odious concessions" to the non-Catholic authorities of the University of Paris; rather, Ozanam informs Dufieux, he risked his career through his efforts to rehabilitate and defend Catholicism in his lectures.

Apparently Ozanam's answer satisfied Dufieux, for their correspondence continued in a friendly, intimate vein. Whether Dufieux ever apologized for his baseless suspicion is not clear, but Ozanam was too kindly, too magnanimous to let this destroy a friendship. Instead, a month or so after his first letter to Dufieux, when the shock of the accusation had worn off, Ozanam wrote to thank his friend for his letter, quoting the words of David to God, "correct me by the voice of a friend."

If an old comrade could accept the charge of heresy against Ozanam, there must have been widespread suspicion of him among those who did not know him personally. Ozanam felt the extent to which these libels had found an audience, for he prepared a public answer as a means of making clear the falseness of the accusation. He did not publish this, however, because he was advised that it would be more charitable not to do so, and because a fight between Catholics might well give scandal to those outside the Church. Consequently, Ozanam lived under a veil of suspicion for the rest of his life, and the question of his orthodoxy pursued him even into the grave. Ozanam's brother, Alphonse, tells us that five years after Frederic's death, the Papal Nuncio to Paris asked him: "You are a theologian, tell me if your brother was really orthodox?"

Certainly nothing is better evidence of the conservative, even reactionary, attitude of the post-1848 Catholic world than the widespread acceptance of a charge of heresy against one such as Ozanam. Here was a pious, ardent man, who gave proof of his religious zeal by his constant dedication to charity, whose writings are permeated through and through with his faith, whose life indeed was given to the defense and promulgation of that faith, and yet an anonymous accusation of heresy receives attention not only from the ignorant, but from those in high places, and most amazingly from friends. How much this doubt concerning his orthodoxy pained Ozanam, already suffering from the collapse of both his personal and public expectations, can only be imagined.

All of this made the years after 1848 a time of trouble for him. If at times he gave way to discouragement, particularly over his ill health which prevented him from continuing his scholarly work, still for the most part, Ozanam maintained his confidence in the future of his Society. The disappointments and anxieties of the post-1848 world did not lead him to despair or to alter radically his view of the present and the future. What they did was to help him to understand better the lot of the individual Christian and of the Church itself here on earth. If he continued to be optimistic, it was now a more Christian optimism in that it included a large dose of temporal pessimism.

Ozanam's optimism was sturdy enough to withstand the storm of 1848 because its roots were deep in his Christianity, for his confidence in the future, his belief in progress, as well as his acceptance of the modern world grew out of a theology of history, out of a great trust in Providence. He understood well that all the events of this world — past, present, and future — are God's plan for man, that each event, no matter how trivial, no matter how evil in itself, is part of this providential design. It was this that gave him a serene assurance that the disasters of his day would ultimately contribute in some way to the destiny of mankind. As he wrote:

> God has not created man without design, and this eternal design, supported by an infinite power, cannot remain without effect. The will that moves the stars rules also the course of civilization. Thus humanity accomplishes a necessary destiny.

That the events of this world happen in accordance with the mysterious will of God is an accepted commonplace of Christianity. Ozanam, however, goes further in that he argues that man can comprehend a part of the providential plan insofar as he can discern a visible, upward progress in history. This progress is moral, not material, and takes place in society as a whole, within humanity. A study of the history of civilization will show this progress, and this indeed was the primary aim of his historical writings: namely, to describe the advance of society through the influence of Christianity. Not only can man discover the evidence of progress in the past, he can also posit it for the future. The path upward may have many twists and turns, but overall mankind advances up the mountain of perfection. The peak, it is true, will never be reached by our earthly society, but progress toward it is not only possible but a part of the providential plan.

This, in brief, is the basis of Ozanam's optimism. Clearly it runs the risk of reducing the supernatural mystery of the effect of Providence in human affairs to a natural, mundane factor whose benefits can be seen and understood in their relation to the world. And in the halcyon days before 1848, when the evidence of improvement in society was before him, Ozanam's expectation of the immediate realization of a great, new Christian age resulted from an oversimplification and secularization of the mystery of the role of Providence. Doubtless he trusted too strongly in the direct, secular benefits of this divine influence.

Although the events of 1848 did not cause him to alter his fundamental concept of the beneficent direction of Providence in human affairs, nevertheless the disasters of that year gave him a more profound, spiritual understanding of this attribute of God.

He continued to insist that Christians must be reconciled to their society if they are to influence it. To reject and to withdraw from society, no matter how desperate the circumstances, can never be a Christian answer. To despair of one's age is to despair of God. "I cannot associate," he asserted, "with those who condemn so bitterly the present age; this is another way of condemning Providence." Instead of despairing in the face of catastrophe the Christian must learn from it. The sorrows and disappointments of this life, believes Ozanam, are given to us in order to teach us to be better, and it is in this light that he viewed the February Revolution and the June Days. "What a stormy epoch, but instructive!" he wrote on one occasion. On another he referred to the "great lesson of 1848" from which Frenchmen must learn if they do not wish God "to strike a second time and harder."

What Ozanam hoped his fellow Catholics would learn from these events was to give their support to democracy and to the cause of the poor, but what he learned personally was a more Christian comprehension of the mystery of Providence. It was not that he gave up his confidence in the progress of society; rather he now saw that the road ahead was long and rocky. No longer does he write of the immediate victory of the good in society, of the triumph of the Church in the modern world, for after 1848 he realized that it is the destiny of the Church and of Christians to struggle, not to triumph.

Progress, in the mature, post-1848 view of Ozanam, is achieved only after a constant struggle between the good and evil elements in each man and in the world as a whole. Because of man's freedom and because of original sin, progress is a battle between two principles in man — perfection and corruption. Hence the advance of society toward perfection is a series of defeats and victories, of retrogression followed by progression, so that Ozanam no longer insists that we can see clearly the evidence of how we progress. The last years, he admits, have robbed him of his hopes, but they have taught him to put his trust in God, not in man. We must await God's judgment upon this world, we must wait with confidence and trust the mysterious secret of Providence. Although we can wait with hope and confidence, still we must realize that it is the destiny of the Church to suffer, not to dominate. It is the Church Militant not the Church Triumphant that Ozanam now stresses. Christ "remained only a moment upon Tabor, we have no image of his Transfiguration; but He passed a day [sic] on the Cross, it is humanity crucified that is upon our altars."

Thus did Ozanam learn from his sorrows and privations. His trust in Providence was not shaken in the least, nor was his confidence in the ultimate, overall moral progress of humanity, but his understanding of Providence and of progress became more Christian, more spiritual under the pressure of crisis. His final statement in this difficult matter was presented in the introduction to *Civilization in the Fifth Century*, written in 1852, a year before his death, in the midst of increasing bad health and at the very time when conservatism was in full power. In it Ozanam reasserts his assurance in the ultimate moral progress of mankind, achieved, however, only after many defeats and by bitter struggle:

> It remains therefore to leave a place for liberty in human destiny, and consequently a place for error and crime. There will be some days of sickness, some lost years, some centuries that do not move forward, some centuries that retrogress. . . . In these periods of disorder God lets the people be masters of their own acts, but He has his hand upon society; He does not permit it to deviate beyond a certain point, and it is there that He awaits it in order to lead it by a painful and shadowy detour to this perfection that they [men] have forgotten for the moment.

Such was the development of Ozanam's thought in the midst of trial and suffering. But the most severe test of his understanding of and trust in Providence was yet to come, for neither the collapse of his hopes for society nor the aura of suspicion which surrounded him can compare to the complete breakdown of his health which also occurred at this time.

Although Ozanam had undergone a serious sickness in his early childhood and was never in what could be called robust health, still his physical condition was hardy enough to sustain years of strenuous, incessant study and research. It was not until 1846, at the age of thirty-three, that his strength failed his will to work. At the end of the academic year of 1846, he was on the verge of a physical and mental collapse. His doctor prescribed a year of rest which Ozanam spent with his wife and daughter traveling in Italy, a pleasant and happy sojourn for him. His health improved with the removal of the strain of teaching and with the joys of visiting in a land full of interest for the scholar and the Catholic.

His stay in Rome, at the height of Pius IX's popularity, was a fitting climax to this satisfactory rest.

Whether this attack in 1846 was a symptom of the kidney ailment that took his life seven years later or the result of overwork is a question that cannot be answered. Very likely it was a combination of the two. Certainly Ozanam's dedication to learning and his strong sense of the obligation to work contributed to his bad health. Possibly if he had possessed a strong constitution, his devotion to his work would not have affected his health. At the same time, it may well be that the kidney disease that struck him down would have made the same disastrous inroads upon his health under any conditions, although it would appear that overwork was a factor in his breakdown in 1846.

That the crisis of 1846 was the advance guard of the fatal disease that eventually brought on his death is probable, since his health was never good after this attack. The years that followed were a gray period of half sickness; fatigue and exhaustion were his constant companions. Still he continued to fulfill his duties, academic or otherwise, which meant a continual drain upon his strength. On several occasions in the period after 1848 he was forced to ease up and to rest. Eventually, at Easter, 1852, he became grievously ill with a high fever and what was diagnosed as pleurisy. His condition became so grave that there was concern for his life. Although he did recover, this was the inception of the fatal illness which led to his death a year and a half later.

The doctors that Ozanam consulted, including his younger brother, Charles, who had chosen this profession, were unable to diagnose his illness. Apparently they feared the scourge of the nineteenth century, consumption, for his recurring fevers and his great weakness would make possible such a conclusion. Be that as it may, they prescribed for him what were the standard treatments of the age for almost all sickness: to drink mineral water and to spend some time in a hot, dry climate. Consequently, in the pursuit of these two health aids, Ozanam spent the last year of his life far away from his beloved Paris, seeking hopelessly for an improvement in his condition. Unfortunately, almost everywhere he and his family traveled in their search for a dry climate, it rained. The winter of 1853, which Ozanam spent near Florence, Italy, was, to judge from Ozanam's letters, a constant flood from the skies. That the climate and rest had little to do with his health is indicated by the ups and downs that he experienced in this period. Despite the rain and the constant travel the fever would disappear for a time and his strength would in some measure return, but this was always followed by a relapse. In January, 1853, after a happy Christmas during which his health was much improved, a new symptom appeared: a swelling of the legs. Still the doctors listened to his chest, recommended digitalis and a dry climate. It was not until later in the year when the swelling became worse that it was decided that his trouble was an infection of the kidney, a diagnosis that was confirmed by a postmortem autopsy.

This long, severe illness was a heavy trial for Ozanam, leaving him restless, worried, and melancholy. Under the best of circumstances and temperaments, a prolonged, increasingly serious illness wears down the spiritual and psychological as well as the physical strength. In Ozanam's case this was especially true, for his was a nervous, sensitive disposition with a tendency to melancholy. Long periods of inactivity and sickness led his active imagination to reflect upon the uncertainty of the future. He was aware of this tendency to anxiety and unease, writing to a friend in these words: "I see everything black when I dream of my lost career, of a sad existence as an invalid and my family abandoned to all the danger of a somber future."

He found particularly trying his inability to continue his scholarly work. This arose in part because of his strong feelings, which were certainly excessive, as to the obligations to work. Thus he wrote in October, 1852, while in the grip of a fatal, enervating sickness:

> The worst is the idleness in which I am obliged to live . . . it is my spirit which fails, and when I come to the end of a day, having done nothing, this uselessness weighs upon me like a remorse, and it seems to me that I did not earn either the bread that I eat nor the bed where I lie.

He was also greatly disturbed because he was forced to halt his work at the point where it was becoming a mature, finished contribution to historical scholarship. He felt as if he were stopped after years of preparation on the threshold of his life's work. A constant source of sorrow to him during his long illness was the thought of the waste of so many years of research and labor, the harvest of which he was now prevented from reaping. Doubtless the consciousness that he had something of value to present in these never-to-be-written volumes, which even one as modest as Ozanam could not help but recognize, added to his sorrow.

Because of all this, also perhaps because of the nature of the disease afflicting him, Ozanam was often restless and disturbed. The greatest strain, the source indeed of many of his other anxieties, was the uncertainty as to his future health. The continual fluctuations in his condition — a period of great improvement when he was sure he was on the road to recovery, only to be followed by a more serious relapse — eroded his spirit. It was the cruel disillusionment of his hopes that was so hard to bear. Each time his health improved, Ozanam joyfully awaited his imminent return to Paris and his work; each time the future gave the lie to his hopes. Here we find the key to much of his restlessness and anxiety; once the worst was certain and his hope for recovery largely gone, Ozanam was able to resign himself to whatever future Providence had in store for him.

He understood this well, for Ozanam had, to an uncommon degree, the faculty of self-analysis. Throughout his life he was able to consider his actions and his interior life with candor and realism. This demands an honesty and a willingness to face unpalatable truths that most men do not possess. In the midst of this last illness, this ability did not desert him, for in his letters to his friends and relatives he was brutally frank about his tendency to discouragement and, in his eyes, his weakness in not overcoming his restlessness. Thus, in a letter to his old friend, J. J. Ampere, written in April, 1853, after his recovery from an almost fatal worsening of his condition, Ozanam very accurately and honestly analyzed his mental state:

> During the last three weeks of Lent, I seriously thought of preparing myself for the last sacrifices. It goes against nature; however, I thought, that with God's help, I was succeeding in detaching myself from everything outside of those who love me and whom I can love elsewhere than here below. . . . Since Easter, I began to recover, and without being entirely well, I can hope for my cure. The evil is that I become attached at the same time to life. In proportion that I think seriously of seeing Paris again, I think of my work, my plans, and, is it necessary to say it? of the judgment of scholars and the public.

As this should make clear, his anxiety, his agitation did not result from an inability to accept God's will; it was the uncertainty of what this will demanded that made it so difficult. Once he knew the destiny that faced him, he was able to reconcile himself to it, indeed to accept it willingly as coming from God. As he wrote in the midst of his sufferings, "I strive to abandon myself with love to the will of God."

At the same time his resignation to God's will, his acceptance of suffering and death, had nothing morbid or neurotic about it. It was not that of a disillusioned, disappointed person who is tired of life, but that of a man full of the joy of his earthly existence. He was still a young man, with a bright, promising career before him, with a happy life: a devoted wife, a loving child, and many close friends and relations. That he should wish to continue to live is only to be expected. Doubtless, as he wrote in the letter to Ampere, it goes against nature to turn one's back on life, but with the help of God, with his deep religious faith, and his understanding of the ultimate spiritual end of man, he was able, in his words, "to make these sacrifices when Providence requires them . . . as it is done in heaven — that is to say, with joy and love."

As the months wore on and his condition worsened, Ozanam meditated upon the spiritual benefits of the sufferings that God had sent him. He wrote in a letter in 1851:

> I admire the order of Providence which does not wish that we should become too much at home here on earth. God has not permitted that I should take root in a comfortable existence.

A couple of years later, when his health was much worse, he used the occasion of the serious illness of a friend to write of the blessings of such a fate. Too humble to suggest openly that he had received such benefits, still Ozanam surely had his own situation in mind:

> What better preparation [for death] than a long sickness and many good works? For me, when I see Christians tested by slow cruel evils, I imagine souls who have had their purgatory in this world, and who have the right to the respectable pity

that we owe to the just of the suffering Church. Ah! if God
wants to accept for the expiation of their sins these pains borne
here below, they will be happy to be purified at this price, by
sorrows infinitely less than those of the other life, in the midst
of the consolations of religion, of friendship, of family. . . .
Suffer thus two years, ten years even, and afterwards to enter
forthwith in the peace of heaven, would this not be the hap-
piest of destinies?

He drew much spiritual sustenance from his reading of
the Bible, finding consolation especially in the Psalms, which
he read over and over again and which he described as "those
sublime pleas, those flights of hope, those supplications full
of love which answer to all needs, to all the distresses of
human nature." In a letter written in May, 1853, three
months before his death, to a Jewish convert to Catholicism
Ozanam pointed out the intimate tie that the Old Testament makes between Judaism and Christianity. Humbly he
exposed how the Psalms gave him the will to overcome his
weakness in the face of suffering:

> The hand of the Lord has touched me, I believe, as Job, as
> Ezechias, as Tobias, not until death but to test me grievously.
> Unhappily. I have not the patience of these just men, I let
> myself be overcome easily by suffering, and I could not console
> myself over my weakness, if I did not find in the Psalms the
> cries of sorrow that David sent forth to God, and to which
> God responds in the end by granting him pardon and peace.

Throughout these bleak months, when his health permitted, Ozanam continued to strive to accomplish what he
considered to be his duty. In that last winter and spring in
Italy, weak and hardly able to walk, he still worked in the
libraries and archives seeking documents upon medieval history. In the spring of 1853, three months before his death,
he put together the notes he had taken the previous year
during a visit he had made to Spain. These were published

as *A Pilgrimage to the Land of the Cid*, his last book before his death. Everywhere that he traveled in the pursuit of health, in southern France and in Italy, he contacted and visited with the local conferences of the St. Vincent de Paul Society. That last year in Italy, when he was literally dying, he managed to address at some length and with great eloquence two newly founded Italian conferences. Appropriately, then, the work of the evening of his life was in those fields in which he had labored since the dawn and through the heat of the day: namely, in the search for truth and in the practice of charity.

By the summer of 1853 it was clear to all, and by now to Ozanam himself, that the end was near. He was no longer able to work and could walk only with great difficulty. His weakness was such that he was forced to remain in bed for most of the time. In September it was decided that he should return to France, so that when death came it would be in his beloved native land. As Ozanam left the house where he had lived these last, agonizing months, he raised his arms to heaven and cried: "My God, I thank You for the suffering and afflictions that You have sent me in this place; accept them as expiation for my sins."

Fortunately the weather was good and the sea calm, so that the voyage to Marseilles was made in good fashion. It had been intended that Ozanam should continue on to Paris, but his weakness was so great that such a journey was out of the question. Surrounded by his family, with all the consolations and assistances of the religion he had served so well, he died on September 8, 1853.

As so often happens, the public recognition of his scholarship and of his virtues, which had not always been given to him during his life, came in profusion after his death. Many of those who knew him published in the months following his death memoirs and testimonials of their admiration and affection for him, while his *Civilization in the Fifth Century*, published posthumously in 1856, was awarded a prize by L'Academie Française.

As a young man Ozanam expressed a thought that can serve as his epitaph: "We are here below in order to accomplish the will of Providence." This was the key to his life and to his thought. It was his trust in Providence that permitted him, in the midst of a stormy century, beset by personal difficulties and sufferings, to remain confident, hopeful, and optimistic. It was his understanding that Providence worked through the liberty of man that led him to insist that Christians must act to overcome the evils in their society if they are to cooperate in the realization of the divine plan. It was the love of God, expressed in the providential care of man, which inspired Ozanam's love for his fellow men, the source of his great contributions in the work of charity. "To accomplish the will of Providence," this was the basis of Ozanam's life from his youth until his last day on earth.

Index

Acton, Lord, 86, 88
Affre, Archbishop, 95, 102, 105;
  death, 115 f
Ampere, Andre, 2 f
Ampere, J. J., 3, 59, 78, 142

Bailly, 13, 21
Ballanche, 2, 12, 83, 131, 133
Blanqui, Louis-Auguste, 99, 110

Cavaignac, General, 111, 116, 118,
  120
Charles X, King, 6 f
Chateaubriand, 4 f, 12, 83, 131, 133
Constitutional Assembly, 107, 109;
  of 1848, 109, 110
Cousin, Victor, 52
Curnier, 24

Dawson, Christopher, 71
de Bourges, Michel, 100
de Coux, Charles, 36
DeMaistre, Joseph, 91, 85
de Melun, Armand, 39, 40, 120, 124
de Quelen, Archbishop, 16, 17, 95
de Tocqueville, Alexis, 86, 99, 105,
  109, 111 f
Dufieux, 132 f

Gerbet, Abbé, 13
Gibbon, Edward, 67
Gregory XVI, Pope, 81
Guizot, 34

Jouffroy, 9, 15
July Monarchy, 98; economic policy,
  34
July Revolution of 1830, 6 f
June Days, 111, 112

Lacordaire, Père, 17 f, 45, 49, 81,
  86, 95, 107, 108

Lallier, 12, 16, 23, 26, 48
Lamennais, Abbé, 10, 81
L'Avenir, 10, 81
Le Correspondent, 101, 120, 123
Ledru-Rollin, 117, 118
Lenormant, 75
L'Ère Nouvelle, 108, 122, 123, 124,
  125
Letaillandier, 21
London Exhibition of 1851, 93
Louis-Philippe, King, 8, 98, 100
L'Univers, 40, 72, 82, 130 ff
Lyon, riots, 1834, 34

Maret, Abbé, 86, 108
Michelet, Jules, 74
Montalembert, Count, 8, 13, 66, 72,
  81, 84, 86, 120

Napoleon, Louis, 118, 119, 129
National Workshops, 110
Noirot, Abbé, 2

Ozanam, Alphonse, 45, 106, 133
Ozanam, Charles, 139
Ozanam, Frederic, attitude toward
  charity, 38, 41 f; belief in progress,
  92 ff; Christian optimism of, 134 ff;
  death, 145; and death of Archbishop Affre, 115; death of parents, 46; his liberal Catholicism,
  79; joins faculty of University of
  Paris, 54; and the June Days, 113 f;
  as a lecturer, 77; liberty, 89; marriage, 55; political philosophy, 85 f;
  separation of Church and State,
  87; socio-economic ideas, 35 ff,
  125 ff; view of Middle Ages, 67

Pius IX, Pope, 118 ff, 123, 128,
  130, 139; election of, 96; flight of,
  98
Poor, life of, 31 ff

Quinet, Edgar, 74

Ravignan, Père, 17, 95
Renan, Ernest, 9, 78
Revolution of 1848, xiv, 40, 98, 105

St. Vincent de Paul Society, 62, 124, 145; attraction to Catholics, 27 ff;

founding of, 20; growth of, 25
Sister Rosalie, 21, 39

Talbot, Monsignor, 29

Veuillot, Louis, 74, 80, 82, 91, 130
Voltaire, 66